Finding
True Love

D1304620

# Finding True Love

## INTERACTIVE DISCOVERY BOOK
## DEVOTIONAL AND JOURNAL

JOSH MCDOWELL

AND

ED STEWART

WORD PUBLISHING
NASHVILLE
A Thomas Nelson Company

Unless otherwise indicated, Scripture quotations used in this book are from the Holy Bible, New International Version (NIV). Copyright © 1973, 1978, 1984, International Bible Society. Used by permission of Zondervan Bible Publishers.

Other Scripture references are from the following sources:

New American Standard Bible (NASB), © 1960, 1977 by the Lockman Foundation.

The Good News Bible: The Bible in Today's English Version (TEV) © 1976 by the American Bible Society.

### Library of Congress Cataloging-in-Publication Data

McDowell, Josh.
    Finding true love : interactive discovery book : devotional and journal for youth / by Josh McDowell and Ed Stewart.
      p. cm.
    ISBN 0-8499-4080-X (pbk.)
    1. Youth—Religious life. 2. Love—Religious aspects—Christianity. 3. Sex—Religious aspects—Christianity. 4. Dating (Social customs)—Religious aspects—Christianity. 5. Youth—Prayer-books and devotions—English. I. Stewart, Ed. II. Title.

BV4639 .M367 2000
248.8'3—dc21

                                         00-024465
                                          CIP

*Printed in the United States of America*

00 01 02 03 04 05 PC 9 8 7 6 5 4 3 2 1

# Finding True Love

## LUKE'S STORY

Luke eased up on the accelerator a little, even though he was secretly anxious to get to the top of the hill. But he slowed the car because his girlfriend, Traci, seated next to him, was enjoying the night view of the city on the gently winding road to the planetarium. And Luke wanted Traci to enjoy the evening because he knew she would make the date more enjoyable for him later if she was happy.

"Look at this, Traci." Luke motioned to the city lights sparkling out his side window. Just as he hoped, Traci leaned toward him as far as her seat belt would allow in order to take in the view. The subtle, sweet fragrance of her hair and skin was delicious. Her left hand touched bare skin at the base of his neck, sending a chill of excitement down his spine. Her right hand rested gently on his thigh. The surge of pleasure tempted him to divert his concentration from the road. But he gripped the wheel determinedly and kept his eyes straight ahead. He didn't want a careless accident to spoil this perfect evening.

"Ooo, it's beautiful, Luke," Traci sang. "Look, you can see the train pulling out of the station down there." Her warm breath brushed his ear, giving him another chill of excitement.

Luke glanced out the window for a half-second. "Yeah, that's neat," he said, even though he never saw the train.

"You're so sweet to bring me up here on such a beautiful night," Traci said. Then she nuzzled him on the cheek with her nose, concluding with a soft peck of a kiss before settling back in her seat. Luke could feel his heartbeat quicken at her closeness. Traci always sparked the greatest feelings in him. He couldn't get enough of her— her looks, her smell, and especially her touch. He was guardedly sure she felt the same way about him.

This had been an expensive evening for Luke. Traci loved romantic dates, so he had treated her to a candlelight dinner at an expensive French restaurant in town. Since it was kind of a dressy evening, he'd also had to spring for a nice shirt and tie. And the planetarium show at the observatory would cost him another huge chunk of change. As a high school senior with a part-time job, Luke could hardly afford such a spendy date.

But when he'd picked up Traci at her house tonight, he'd known the expense was worthwhile. She looked more like a movie star than a high school junior in a dress that accentuated her drop-dead figure. She was worth every minute of overtime he would put in next week to replenish his wallet.

"Tell me about the planetarium show at the observatory again," Traci cooed, gently caressing Luke's upper leg. "I can't believe I have lived in town almost a year now and have never been up here."

"The planetarium theater has a large, domed ceiling," Luke explained, trying to keep his mind off Traci's hand on his leg. "When the lights are turned off, a special projector fills the dome with specks of light. It looks just like the sky at midnight, full of stars and planets.

The narrator points out the major stars and constellations. There are asteroids and shooting stars. It's really cool."

"I love astronomy. I can't wait," Traci said with a cute little laugh. "The stars are so romantic." Luke smiled to himself. As long as Traci felt romantic, he was sure to have a good time.

It was chilly on top of the hill, so Luke wrapped his arm around Traci as they hurried from the parking lot to the planetarium theater. There were at least two hundred people watching the program, Luke figured, but he noticed no one but Traci. She seemed to enjoy the presentation, and Luke enjoyed being close to her, relishing the softness of her hand in his. Encouraged by her closeness, he stole an occasional kiss in the darkness, and Traci responded warmly.

After the show, they strolled to a bench outside where they could see the city lights. Luke draped his jacket around Traci's shoulders and wrapped her in his arms. Alone on the bench, huddled with Traci to stay warm, Luke's desire for her heated up. Her willingness spurring him on, Luke's kisses became more passionate than ever before. The pleasure was intense, and he just wanted to be closer to her. Traci's response told him she wanted the same thing.

Once they returned to the car and resumed their romantic cuddling, Luke could hardly keep himself under control. As a Christian, he understood the importance of sexual purity. He had promised God at youth camp three years earlier that he would remain a virgin until he was married, and he had kept his promise through high school. But his vow had never really been tested until he'd met Traci Lockhart two months earlier. His feelings for her were so strong, not like anything he had felt for other girls. It was a hunger that just seemed to grow more intense with every date.

Swept up in the emotion of the moment, Luke smothered Traci with kisses. Yielding to the urgency he sensed, he touched and caressed her in ways he never had before. Traci seemed so willing, so receptive for the affection Luke yearned to shower on her. It took all the will power he could muster to stop before breaking his promise to God. "We had better get home," he said, pulling away from her reluctantly.

"Yeah, I guess so," Traci said timidly.

They drove home in silence. Luke felt embarrassed for being so bold in his physical approach to Traci, but he seemed almost driven. Why did he feel more strongly toward Traci than any other girl he'd dated? Why did he feel so compelled to have sex with her? As the car wound down the hill toward the city, the thought occurred to him for the first time: *My desire for Traci is so strong I must really be in love with her.*

## TRACI'S STORY

*Forgive me, God, for compromising my standards,* Traci prayed silently as Luke drove her home. She was ashamed about her behavior, seemingly on the verge of breaking her vow of purity to God. Traci had never intended to go all the way with Luke or any other boy before marriage. But she had been swept away by her emotions tonight. The romantic dinner, the candles, the stars, Luke's eagerness to make her feel special—everything seemed so right. He had been so sweet and affectionate to her, she would have done anything to please him.

Then, for some reason, Luke stopped before it was too late. Traci was very relieved, but she was also a little disappointed. He was so abrupt that she wondered now if she had done something wrong. *Did he stop because I was too willing? Was I not willing enough? Did I do something that turned him off? Was he disappointed because I didn't measure up to other girls he has dated?* These questions nagged at Traci during the silent ride home. She hoped this would not be their last time together; she did not want to lose this great guy.

Traci flashed on their first meeting—at a weekend ski retreat for the high school group from the church Luke attended. Traci, who went to a much smaller church across town, signed up at the invitation of Polly, a friend from school who attended Luke's church. Traci had noticed Luke as soon as she'd arrived at the church. He was a leader in the high school group, welcoming students at the registration table in the parking lot and handing out bus and cabin assignments. Luke was not only nice to her, a first-time visitor; he was nice to everyone and working hard to get the retreat off to a positive start. And he was too cute for words!

Traci was quietly elated when Luke ended up on her bus, sitting only a couple of rows away. During the three-hour drive up the mountain, Traci's attention was divided between chatting with Polly and her friends and secretly watching Luke and his friends, who were having even more fun. Traci admired from a distance his wit and humor, and she was impressed with his respect for the adult leaders and his ability to help everyone have a good time. He led their busload of students in prayer for travel safety and for spiritual and relational growth during the retreat. This was a quality Christian guy, Traci realized, and she wanted to get to know him better.

The weekend afforded so many "unplanned" opportunities to get acquainted that Traci suspected Luke may have noticed her too. He and his friend Curtis showed up at her breakfast table Saturday morning. While Curtis kept Polly occupied, Luke peppered her with questions: How did you find out about our church and the retreat? What is your church like? How long have you been a Christian? How long have you been skiing? What do you plan to do after high school? It was obvious Luke was not like most of the guys she knew. He asked questions about her instead of bragging about himself or trying to impress her with his macho accomplishments. He was interested in her spiritual life. He was courteous, and he actually had table manners. Before that weekend, Traci had never before met an eighteen-year-old boy she considered a gentleman. She ate her breakfast slowly because she did not want their first conversation to end.

That afternoon on the slopes, Traci encountered Luke several times. He was a good skier and she was not, so he offered a few helpful pointers, without embarrassing her for her limited ability and experience. Luke happened along a few times when Traci fell, helping her up and making sure she was not hurt. And that afternoon in the lodge he appeared with a cup of steaming hot chocolate as she sat by the fire drying her socks and warming her feet. She was bothered that the strange numbness in her hands had flared up again, but she didn't mention it to Luke. They talked for more than an hour, time Luke could have spent skiing. Traci was enthralled. Luke was so kind, so sweet, so polite, so helpful. She could not believe he was paying attention to her when practically any girl on the mountain would have jumped at the chance to be with him.

Preparing for the Saturday night bus ride home, Traci arranged to leave the seat next to her empty, hoping Luke would sit there when he was finished with the announcements and prayer. He did, and Traci was secretly ecstatic. They talked for three hours, while most of the kids on the bus slept. They shared with each other how they came to Christ, their dreams for the future, their favorite foods, movies, and music. Traci couldn't believe how much they had in common. Just before they pulled into the church parking lot, Luke asked her out for the next weekend. She accepted immediately, intent on canceling anything on her calendar that might keep her from being with Luke.

The two months from that night to tonight had been magical, Traci assessed. Luke treated her like a princess. Their first date had been a picnic by the lake, with Luke fixing the lunch and providing soft music on his boom box. He took her to movies—the romantic kind she liked instead of car-exploding, gun-blazing guy movies. He took her to a play at the performing arts center. They took long walks together downtown and out in the country. They laughed and sang together and even prayed together. On their third date Luke had kissed Traci for the first time, and she'd stayed awake half the night thinking how special she felt to be his girlfriend.

Luke was ever the perfect gentleman—a real-life Prince Charming. He brought flowers to her. He opened doors for her and seated her at tables. He called; he sent her cards and notes. They kissed and embraced often and held hands most of the time they were together. But Luke had never emphasized the physical side of their relationship—until tonight.

Luke stopped the car in front of Traci's house and, as always, hurried around to her side to open the door. As soon as she stepped out, she was face to face with him in the cool night air.

"Traci, I'm . . . I'm sorry about tonight," Luke stammered. "I mean . . . I just . . . felt so close to you . . ." his voice trailed off, and Traci knew he was having trouble saying what he meant.

"It's all right, Luke," she said reassuringly. "You're so sweet, I know you didn't mean to do anything wrong. I'm glad we stopped. Thank you."

After several silent seconds he said, "Is it OK if I call you tomorrow?"

Traci smiled. "I was hoping you would."

After being kissed lightly on the cheek, Traci went inside. Standing at the window, she watched Luke drive away. *Even tonight he was the perfect gentleman,* she thought dreamily, *apologizing for his passionate advance, asking permission to call me. I forgave him, and I can't wait to talk to him tomorrow. Luke and I have something very special. It must be . . . true love.*

## TIME OUT TO CONSIDER

Traci and Luke have only been dating two months. But love—the big L-word—is already on their minds. It's no wonder they are thinking about love, since we live in a love-crazed culture. Love is the predominant theme in so many of our popular songs, movies, novels, and TV programs. Everywhere you look in the world of entertainment someone is either falling into love, falling out of love, making love, faking love, giving love, needing love, living in love, or dying for love.

In the real world, life without love is the pits. The yearning to love and be loved by someone is as common in the human family as heartbeat and breath. Everyone seems to crave true love, a love that is strong and deep, a love that will last for all time. Yet the pursuit of love has caused more heartache and pain, more brokenness and bitterness, than all the diseases and wars in history.

What is this thing called love, and how do you know when you have found it? People like Traci and Luke are willing to give almost anything to experience love, particularly from the opposite sex. Love makes the world go 'round, we say. Yet so many students searching for love find only heartache and disappointment because they don't know what they are looking for. They confuse true love with other experiences and emotions. As a result, they fail to experience love because they don't know what love *is* and what love *isn't*.

Perhaps you identify with Traci or Luke. You are in a relationship with someone very special and the L-word is on your mind if not in your vocabulary. Are you "in love"? Do you know how to tell if you are? Or maybe you haven't found that someone special yet, but you want to be ready when you do. You want to know what true love is so you can recognize it when it happens in your life.

The first step to identifying true love is to see what true love *isn't*.

*True love is not the same as lust.* Love and lust are often confused in our culture. In fact, many of today's movies, popular songs, and novels about love are really about lust. How can you tell the difference? Love gives; lust takes. Love values; lust uses. Love endures; lust subsides. Luke may be a little confused between the two. He enjoys being close to Traci because she awakens his pleasurable sexual urges and feelings. He does nice things for Traci at least in part

because he thinks it will make her more willing to share the physical closeness and intimacy that he enjoys. And his lust nearly caused him to compromise his sexual purity and hers.

Yes, physical attraction is often the spark that eventually ignites into true love. God designed us with the desire and capacity for sexual intimacy. But if your interaction with someone of the opposite sex is based on intense sexual feelings and physical gratification, lust may be playing the role of love in the relationship.

*Love is not the same as romance.* When Luke and Traci were together, they could almost hear violins playing sweet love music. When they kissed, emotional fireworks went off inside. Whenever Luke spoke sweet words of love and affection or cared for Traci in kind, romantic ways, she felt like a princess. Whenever Traci gazed lovingly into his eyes, Luke felt stronger and more important than anyone else. Candlelight dinners, soft music, and starry skies brought on intense romantic feelings in both of them, especially Traci.

Romantic feelings are wonderful in a close male-female relationship. God wired us to experience these feelings in special relationships with the opposite sex. Perhaps you have enjoyed the inner warmth and fireworks of romance in a dating relationship. But the excitement and warmth of romance cannot be equated with love. Romance is a feeling; true love is much more.

*True love is not the same as infatuation.* Infatuation is a fascination with and intense interest in someone of the opposite sex. You find yourself thinking about that person all day and dreaming about him or her at night. You plan your day around seeing or talking to that special person. Your thoughts may be so preoccupied with that person that you can't concentrate on anything else. Another term for infatuation is puppy love. Puppy love may be real to a puppy, but if the only love you experience is puppy love, you will end up living a dog's life!

When people talk about "falling in love" or "love at first sight,"

they are usually talking about infatuation. Infatuation left Traci feeling breathless and starry-eyed about Luke. And Luke sometimes felt lightheaded and addlebrained being with Traci. Maybe you have experienced similar feelings about someone of the opposite sex. Infatuation is not wrong, but it should not be mistaken for love. Infatuation is usually "me-centered"; love is "other-centered."

*True love is not the same as sex.* Many students (and many adults as well) confuse the intensity of sexual desire with true love. It happened to Luke after his sexual hunger for Traci nearly caused him to abandon his promise to remain pure. His strong desire to experience sex with her caused him to wonder if his feelings were based on true love. Perhaps you have wondered the same thing about your sexual desires for someone.

Sex as God intended it is not wrong. It was designed by God for procreation and fulfillment within the bounds of marriage. But sex and love are distinct. You can have sex without love and love without sex. Love is a process; sex is an act. Love is learned; sex is instinctive. Love requires constant attention; sex takes no effort. Love takes time to develop and mature; sex needs no time to develop. Love requires emotional and spiritual interaction; sex requires only physical interaction. Love deepens a relationship; sex without love dulls a relationship.

"If love is more than lust, romance, infatuation, or sex," you may wonder, "how do I know if I'm in love?" That's the big question, especially when you find yourself attracted to members of the opposite sex and increasingly involved in dating. In order to answer that question, you need to know more than what true love *isn't*. You need to understand what true love *is*.

Just as many people confuse love with lust, romance, infatuation, and sex, many are also in the dark about the different kinds of love people express. There are basically three ways of behaving in relationships that people routinely label as "love."

"*I love you if . . .*" Qualified love, *if* love, is *conditional* love. It

is given or received only when certain conditions are met. The only way to get this kind of love is to earn it by performing in an approved way. Some parents love their children *if* they behave well, *if* they get good grades, *if* they act or dress a certain way. Among married or dating couples, love may be withheld *if* one partner fails to do or be what the other expects. *If* love is basically selfish. It is a bargaining chip offered in exchange for something desired.

Many young women have only experienced the kind of love that says, "I love you *if* you give me what I want sexually" or "I love you *if* you have sex with me just once." Another subtle sexual "if" pressure is found in the common misconception that all dating couples are having sex. The message is, "Since everyone is doing it, you will love me if you do it too." What these girls don't realize is that the love they expect to win from a boy by meeting his sexual demands is only a cheap imitation of love intended to compromise their character. It cannot satisfy the need for love, and it is never worth the price of sexual compromise.

*If* love always has strings attached. As long as certain conditions prevail, the relationship is fine. But when expectations are not met, love is withdrawn. Many marriages break up because they were built on *if* love. When one or both partners fail to perform up to the desired standard, "love" turns to disappointment and resentment.

Luke's "love" for Traci at this point may be largely based on *if* love. As long as Traci makes him feel good, as long as she dresses to please him, as long as she allows him to enjoy her closeness, he is interested in her. But what would happen to Luke's "love" if Traci said, "No more kissing, no more hand holding, and certainly no more intense cuddling in the car"? Would he still want to be with her and spend his hard-earned money to show her a good time?

*If* love is not true love. If you are in a relationship where you sense pressure to perform in a certain way to gain the love you desire, the relationship is not governed by true love.

*"I love you because . . ."* The second kind of love, *because* love, is a close cousin to *if* love. One person loves another because of something he or she is, has, or does. Someone may say, "I love you because you are so beautiful" or "I love you because you take good care of me" or "I love you because you make me laugh." Traci may be an example of *because* love, since she is strongly attracted to Luke because he is so sweet, kind, and romantic around her.

*Because* love sounds pretty good. Almost everyone appreciates being loved for who they are or what they do. It is certainly preferable to *if* love, which must be constantly earned and requires a lot of effort. Being loved because we are good looking, witty, kind, wealthy, popular, and so on seems much less demanding and conditional than trying to bargain for love.

But what will happen to Traci's love when she meets someone who is sweeter and kinder than Luke? How will she treat Luke if he stops being an impressive youth group leader or if he cannot afford to take her on romantic dates? If Traci's love is based on what Luke does, it may not survive any negative changes in his role or performance.

*Because* love is not true love. You may find yourself attracted to someone because of his or her personality, position, intelligence, skill, or ability. But if your love is not founded on more than what that person appears to be, has, or does, it will not last.

*"I love you, period."* The third kind of love is love without conditions. This kind of love says, "I love you despite what you may be like deep down inside. I love you no matter what might change about you. You can't do anything to turn off my love. I love you, period!"

*Love, period* is not blind. It can and should know a great deal about the other person. It may be aware of that person's failures, shortcomings, and faults. Yet it totally accepts him or her without demanding anything in return. There is no way you can earn this type of love, nor can you lose it. It has no strings attached.

*Love, period* is different from *if* love in that it does not require certain conditions to be met before it is given. It is also different from *because* love in that it is not generated by attractive or desirable qualities in the other person. Lust, romance, infatuation, sex, *if* love, and *because* love are predominantly about getting something from another person. True love is about giving to another person. Luke and Traci are still closer to the getting side in their relationship. If what they identify as love is to grow into true love, each of them will need to make a transition to the giving side.

## LUKE'S STORY

Luke tugged at the bill of his batting helmet and settled his feet into the batter's box. After a couple of practice swings with the aluminum bat, he called out, "OK, Doug, I'm ready."

Doug Shaw stood outside the batting cage with the coins Luke had given him. At Luke's words, he dropped them into the machine to activate the mechanical pitcher sixty feet from where Luke stood coiled and ready. In a few seconds, it hurled the first baseball toward the center of the strike zone. Luke whipped the bat around to meet it. *Thwang!* The ball shot to the netting high above the mechanical arm and tumbled harmlessly to the cement floor.

"Nice rip, Luke," Doug called out. "It would have been a double deep in the gap, no question."

Doug Shaw and his wife Jenny were the volunteer youth sponsors at the church Luke attended. Doug and Luke had just come from a Saturday morning planning breakfast for student leaders in the high school ministry. As fans of sports in general and baseball in particular, they tried to get to the batting cages once or twice a month together.

The second pitch streaked toward the plate. Luke's swing barely ticked the ball. He missed the next two pitches completely.

"You're uppercutting, man," Doug said. "Level out your swing. Drive the ball instead of trying to loft it."

Luke grunted his acknowledgment, then connected with the next pitch.

"Great swing—another double," Doug said, clapping his hands.

After they had worked up a sweat taking cuts in the cage, Doug and Luke bought cans of soda and sat down at a nearby picnic table in the sunshine to drink them. Their conversation was punctuated by the *clink* of baseballs making contact with aluminum bats in the batting cages.

When their discussion of baseball had played out, Doug said, "I notice that you have been spending time with the new girl from Madison High, Traci Lockhart."

Luke studied the top of his can of Dr. Pepper. "Yeah, I have," he said without much expression.

"She seems like a nice girl—very sharp upstairs, very sweet."

Luke nodded. "Traci is really special," he said.

Doug evaluated the response. "You don't sound very enthused. Is everything all right, I mean with you and Traci?"

Luke blew a long sigh. "I guess I'm supposed to talk to you about it."

"What do you mean?"

Luke took another drink. "Well, I'm not sure how it's going with Traci and me. I prayed last night that if I God wanted me to talk to somebody, you would ask about Traci today. Do you mind if I tell you about our relationship and ask you a few questions?"

"Not at all, Luke," Doug said. "I'm always glad to hear what you have to say, and I'll share what I can."

Luke related his account of meeting Traci during the ski retreat. He explained how he'd assigned himself to Traci's bus just to be near her, and that he'd gone out of his way to talk to her during the weekend. He described a few of their dates and how close he and Traci had become in just two months. Doug, chuckling, complimented Luke on his ambition and ingenuity. Luke smiled.

Then he quickly sobered. Speaking softly and haltingly, he told about taking Traci to the planetarium last weekend. Omitting the embarrassing details, he summarized how close he had come to breaking his vow of sexual purity. He admitted that he was wrong to take advantage of Traci as he did. By the time he finished his story, Luke seemed on the verge of crying.

"Luke, I can see that your experience last weekend has caused you a lot of anxiety and concern," Doug said. "I feel that with you, my friend, because I love you. And I'm proud of you for doing the right thing in the end." He added an affectionate but manly pat on the shoulder.

"Thanks," Luke said. "I was pretty sure you would understand."

"So where are you and Traci now?" Doug went on. "Did she break up with you?"

"That's the crazy thing about it," Luke returned. "She was glad we didn't . . . you know . . . go all the way. But she's not mad at me or blaming me for what happened. We talked on the phone a couple of times this week, and she wants to keep going out—double dates, we both agreed."

"And how do you feel about Traci after your experience?" Doug said.

Luke brushed a fly away from his ear. "I'm not sure how I feel, Doug. I want to ask you about it."

"Fire away."

"I've never had such strong feelings for a girl before," Luke explained. "I just want to be with Traci all the time. When we are together, I want to touch her and kiss her, and those desires almost got me in big trouble last weekend. Does this mean I'm . . . in love with Traci?"

"The big L-word," Doug said with a slight smile.

"The word love never crossed my mind with other girls I've dated," Luke explained. "Traci is different. I just want to know if it really is love."

15

"How do *you* think a person knows he or she is in love?" Doug asked.

Luke shrugged. "It's some kind of very special feeling, I guess."

"Let me put it another way. What do you think being in love looks like?"

Luke waved at the fly again. "I don't know. Maybe it looks like two people holding hands, going places together . . ."

Doug pulled a slim, leather-bound New Testament from the back pocket of his jeans. "When I first met Jenny in college, I would have answered those questions the same way you did," he said, flipping through pages. "I want to read to you two verses that really helped me understand what true love is. They're in Ephesians five—verses twenty-eight and twenty-nine."

Doug found the right page and began to read. "'Husbands ought to love their wives as—'"

"Whoa, hold on, Doug," Luke interrupted. "We're talking about the L-word here, not the M-word. I'm not a husband, and I don't plan to be one soon. Marriage with Traci is not in my vocabulary, at least not yet. I need to figure out if I love her first."

"Relax, my friend," Doug said, laughing, "I'm not trying to herd you to the altar. I just want you to see God's definition of true love. In these verses, love just happens to be applied to husbands and wives. It works in all relationships."

Luke thought for a moment. "Well, OK," he said at last.

Doug started over. "'Husbands ought to love their wives as their own bodies. He who loves his wife loves himself. After all, no one ever hated his own body, but he feeds and cares for it, just as Christ does the church.'"

"I thought Christians were supposed to love others *more* than themselves," Luke said.

"We are to love *God* more than we love ourselves," Doug clarified. "But according to Christ's Great Commandment in Matthew twenty-two, we are to love our *neighbor* as we love *ourselves*. And 'neighbor' includes everyone: parents, brothers and sisters, boyfriend or girlfriend, husband or wife."

"But is it right to love ourselves?" Luke pressed. "I mean, isn't that being kind of self-centered?"

"Paul's not talking about people being selfish or self-centered here," Doug explained. "But we all take care of our own basic needs, like getting enough to eat, getting enough sleep, wearing seat belts and driving carefully, and spending time in the Word to grow. Paul says we should care for the needs of others just as we do for ourselves. In fact, you can tell that love is real when the happiness, health, and spiritual growth of another person is as important to you as your own."

Luke cocked his head. "The way you talk about it, love isn't a feeling at all. Love is a way of treating people—caring for them as you do yourself."

Doug nodded. "Strong feelings of attraction—like you describe between you and Traci—are often called love because that's how it's portrayed in movies, TV, and music. Good feelings may accompany love, but true love can happen with or without feelings because love is the activity of caring for a person as you care for yourself."

Luke and Doug talked for another twenty minutes, and Doug led them in a brief prayer. Then Doug left to change clothes and relieve his wife, Jenny, at the quick-print shop they owned and operated together. Luke had to leave too; he'd promised Traci he would take her to buy a battery for her car. Before they parted, Doug issued Luke a specific challenge to apply their discussion in his relationship with Traci. Luke had no idea that Doug's challenge would soon be put to a severe, unexpected test.

## TRACI'S STORY

Traci and her mother had cried off and on since their family doctor's phone call earlier in the morning. Dr. Duncan did not usually talk to patients on Saturday mornings, but today was an exception, he had said. Traci had seen him Friday about the occasional, bothersome numbness in her hands. She had thought little of the symptoms, but her mother had made an appointment just to check it out. The doctor had deemed it important to call with his preliminary diagnosis.

"Multiple sclerosis?" Traci said to her mother, who had taken the call from the doctor. "I've heard of it, but what is it?"

Jackie Lockhart fought back tears as she explained. "It's a disease of the central nervous system, honey, attacking the brain and spinal cord. They don't know the cause, and they don't know the cure. Depending on the locality of the disease, it can produce . . . disabilities." Jackie could no longer hold back the tears.

"Disabilities? What disabilities?" Traci had demanded, suddenly feeling very afraid. "Mom, what's wrong with me? What's going to happen to me?"

It took Traci's mother several minutes to get through the explanation, interrupted by moments of tears shared with her daughter. Jackie tried to encourage her—and herself—by stating that the symptoms can come and go, disappearing for months or years at a time. But unless a cure was found or God miraculously intervened, Traci might eventually lose the use of her legs, arms, speech, or other physical abilities. In response to Traci's direct question, Jackie admitted that MS can eventually be fatal.

Drying her eyes, Traci went out to the front porch to wait for Luke. It was so sweet and kind of him to help her buy a car battery. In the meantime, Jackie put in a call to her ex-husband to tell him the bad news. Traci's father lived in another state with his second wife.

Sitting on the porch and staring aimlessly, Traci wondered how Luke would take her news. She had never told him about the numbness in her hands for a couple of reasons. First, until today, the condition was more a bother to her than a worry, so she didn't think it important to mention. Second, Luke was such a great guy, she wanted to do everything she could to impress him. So volunteering information about her "faults" at this early stage of their relationship had seemed unthinkable.

Now she had to tell him. If she didn't, someone else eventually would, and that would be worse. Besides, it was the right thing to do. As much as she feared that the reality of MS might drive Luke away, the only loving thing to do was to tell him. And she did want to do the loving thing with Luke because she was pretty sure she loved him. The question plaguing her as she watched for his car was, *Does Luke love me enough to stay with me in spite of what I will tell him?* Behind this question was another she did not want to think about at all: *Does Luke even love me?*

As soon as Luke's car pulled up to the curb, Traci ran to it and jumped in. He noticed her red eyes right away. "You've been crying," Luke said with obvious concern. "Traci, what's wrong?"

Traci blurted out the news along with another wave of warm tears. She felt very ugly crying in front of Luke, but she couldn't help it. It didn't seem to matter anyway. The fact that she was not very pretty when she cried was minor in light of the fact that she may be disabled someday.

Luke's response was more than Traci could have hoped for. She would not have been surprised if he had backed away from her as if she had leprosy, saying something like, "Have a nice life," and leaving her standing on the curb. After all, a guy as good looking and sweet as Luke could find a dozen girls without disabilities to go out with by tonight. But instead, he touched her gently and listened intently as she tearfully told him about the disease. He comforted her and encouraged her with caring words. He asked if there was anything he could do for her. And he promised to stick with her through this tough trial.

Then he helped Traci get her feet on the ground again by taking her to the auto parts store to buy the car battery. After installing the battery and giving Traci a tender kiss, he left.

Only later did she begin to wonder if she had seen the last of Luke. Had he been kind, caring, and helpful just long enough to make his escape? Was he even now plotting how to extricate himself from this relationship? Or was Luke's concern as genuine as it had seemed? Did he know even more about love than what he had shown her in the past two months?

## TIME OUT TO CONSIDER

Luke was better prepared to receive Traci's startling revelation thanks to a timely visit with his youth sponsor, Doug Shaw. They didn't know it at the time, but the challenge Doug issued to Luke would be put to a severe test the moment Luke arrived at Traci's house. Doug's challenge was simple enough: Since you are attracted to Traci and she is attracted to you, why not focus your attention on exercising God's definition of love in your relationship?

What is God's definition of love? *Love, period* is the only real love, the only true love, the only biblical love. It is the kind of love God displays toward us: unconditional, no *if,* no *because.* The Bible declares: "God so loved the world that he gave his one and only Son" (John 3:16); "This is love: not that we loved God, but that he loved us and sent his Son as an atoning sacrifice for our sins" (1 John 4:10); "But God demonstrates his own love for us in this: While we were still sinners, Christ died for us" (Rom. 5:8). This is the God who loves us unconditionally, in spite of our sin, in spite of our weakness.

According to the verses Doug read to Luke outside the batting cages, true, unconditional love is evident when the happiness, health, and spiritual growth of another person is as important to you as your own. Paul wrote to the Ephesians, "No one ever hated his own flesh, but nourishes and cherishes it, just as Christ also does the church" (Eph. 5:29 NASB). It is not selfish or self-centered to nourish and cherish our own bodies; it is a natural, healthy love of self. True love means to nourish and cherish another just as we naturally do for ourselves.

To nourish means to nurture toward growth and maturity. For example, in order to nurture a plant or flower in your garden, you provide all the sun, water, and plant food it needs to grow tall and become fruitful. In a similar way, nurturing that special someone in your life means to provide for his or her growth and maturity by meeting needs, just as you make sure your own needs are met.

To cherish means to protect from harm. Picture a mother bird spreading her wings over her babies to shield them from bad weather or danger. Cherishing your special friend means protecting him or her from all harm, just as you take precautions to protect yourself from dangers of any kind.

Here is one of the simplest definitions for true love you will ever find: to protect and provide for another person. It reflects God's picture of love in the Bible. And the supreme example is Jesus Christ's love for the church. He is alive today protecting and providing for us.

What does true love look like in a dating relationship? You will speak and act in ways that protect and provide for your special friend. For example, you will drive carefully instead of recklessly because you want to protect your date from an accident. You will provide activities that will be personally enriching and enjoyable for your friend instead of those of questionable value. And you will not pressure your date to meet your sexual desires but instead protect him or her from the pain of moral compromise.

As you can see, true love from God's perspective is much more than an attraction to or warm feelings about someone special. True love is a *decision,* an *action,* a *response* to care for others as you do yourself. Protecting and providing for others is an act of the will regardless of our feelings. This is how we are to love everyone: family members, friends, classmates, neighbors, even strangers. We should be constantly seeking the happiness, health, and spiritual growth of others, beginning with those closest to us—family members and close friends—and working out to people we don't even know, such as people around the world who benefit from our charitable giving.

If there is a special friend in your life, he or she belongs in that inner circle. If you are learning how to protect and provide for anyone, it should be the one to whom you are most deeply attracted. The relationship may have begun by focusing on infatuation, romantic attachment, or even sex. You may have recognized large doses of *I love you if . . .* or *I love you because . . .* in the way you treat one another. Conditional love rarely protects or provides for another.

If you want the relationship to grow and succeed in God's terms, focus on applying God's definition of love: *I love you, period!* This unconditional love seeks to protect and provide for the other person. Consciously make your friend's happiness, health, and spiritual growth as important to you as your own. If you are in a romantic relationship, you will know it is true love when your heart's desire is to protect and provide for the object of your affection.

Traci's shocking news about MS has sobered Luke and challenged him to reevaluate their relationship. A few hours after being with Traci, Luke found himself seeking out his spiritual mentors, armed with more questions.

## LUKE'S STORY

Luke sat in his car outside the quick-print shop until almost 6:00 P.M. He approached the door just as Jenny Shaw was coming to lock it and flip the window sign from OPEN to CLOSED. The concern on his face must have been as obvious as a blinking neon sign. "Hi, Luke," Jenny said as he approached the door. "Is something wrong?"

"Can I talk to you and Doug for a minute?" he said.

"Of course, Luke. Come on in." Jenny locked the door behind them and led Luke back to the office where Doug was shutting down a computer.

Luke poured out the story of Traci's recently discovered disease. Doug and Jenny were shocked, saying they would stop by Traci's house on their way home from work.

"I understand a lot more about love since we talked together this morning, Doug," Luke went on. "And I accepted your challenge to begin showing true love to Traci. But I didn't expect this. I mean, Traci is a beautiful girl, but in time her disease could change that. She may not be able to ski or swim or go biking. And if we get married someday—I'm not saying we're going to, but if we do—will she be able to have sex and bear children? I know true love says 'I love you, period,' but I didn't know that period would be so huge."

Doug and Jenny put their hands on their young friend's shoulders. "This has been a tough day for you, Luke," Jenny said, "and we're so sorry about the disappointment you are facing. We will be praying for you as well as for Traci."

"Thanks. That means a lot to me."

Then Doug said, "Only God knows the future, Luke. Only He knows if you and Traci are destined to spend your lives together as husband and wife. That's something you can leave in God's hands because it's in the future. In the meantime, are you still attracted to Traci, I mean, beyond the physical attraction?"

Luke paused only a moment before answering. "Of course. Traci is a special person. She's fun, smart, happy, and we have so much in common. I admit that her appearance got my attention first. But there is a lot more to Traci than how she looks."

"It sounds like Traci means a lot to you," Jenny put in.

Luke nodded. "Yes, a lot."

"Then you have nothing to lose by making Traci's happiness,

health, and spiritual growth as important to you as your own. Loving her God's way will make the most of your relationship right now. And if, in God's plan and timing, you and Traci marry someday, your relationship will be based on true love, not an earthly substitute."

Luke pondered the words for several moments. "OK, but how? Can you give me some practical examples of what my love for Traci can look like, especially in light of what she found out today?"

Doug and Jenny spent the next few minutes offering suggestions. When they all stood to leave, Luke hugged and thanked both of them. He told them he was heading back over to Traci's house for a while. The couple said they would see him there after they got the store buttoned up for the night.

Before leaving the shopping center, Luke stopped at the card shop to buy a card for Traci. He selected one he thought she would like, not a mushy, romantic card, but one with a pretty floral design and blank space inside to write.

He wrote only a few quick lines, knowing there would be many other cards, notes, and conversations in the future: "Traci, you are a wonderful person. I know you can get through this trial. I will be here to help you every step of the way." He rolled the pen in his fingers for several seconds before writing the final two words. They had much more significance to him now, so he wrote them with confidence: "Love, Luke."

## TIME OUT TO CONSIDER

What does true love look like in a boyfriend-girlfriend relationship? It has the same basic elements as love expressed in any other relationship, though elements of affection and time commitment may be greater in this special relationship. Here are a few examples.

*Committed to protect and provide, true love seeks to meet*

*needs for comfort, support, and encouragement.* This was the first thing Doug and Jenny mentioned to Luke when he asked for practical suggestions on showing true love. Everybody needs comfort, support, and encouragement, especially during the inevitable times of pain and discouragement in life. Comfort is not a "pep talk," urging another person to hang in there, tough it out, or hold it together. Comfort is not an attempt to explain why bad things happen to people. Comfort is not a bunch of positive words about God being in control and everything being OK. All of these things may be good and useful in time, but they do not fill the primary need for comfort.

People receive comfort when we feel their hurt and sorrow with them so they know they are not suffering alone. Paul instructed us, "Rejoice with those who rejoice; mourn with those who mourn" (Rom. 12:15). Jenny instructed Luke to comfort Traci and her mother by offering a gentle touch, a tender embrace, and a shoulder to cry on. When your special friend is hurting for some reason, share words like, "I know it hurts," "I'm so sorry you have to go through this," or "I really hurt for you." Save your words of advice or admonitions from Scripture until you have shared your friend's feelings. That's biblical comfort.

True love also meets the need for support. You provide support when you attempt to lighten your friend's load in practical, helpful ways. Acts of support fulfill Paul's instruction in Galatians 6:2: "Carry each other's burdens, and in this way you will fulfill the law of Christ." Luke may have opportunities to perform a number of helpful tasks for Traci and her mother that will help ease their burden in practical ways. You express biblical love to your special friend whenever you serve him or her in practical, helpful ways.

Everybody needs encouragement in life, and true love looks for ways to meet that need. We encourage others whenever we do or say something thoughtful to lift their spirits. The card Luke is taking to Traci, especially the encouraging words he wrote inside, is a simple way of expressing encouragement. You can supply encouragement to others in many practical ways: cards, notes, e-mails, phone calls. Encouragement is communicated when you focus your words and attention on your special friend and any struggles he or she is going through.

*True love does not take advantage of another person.* Using someone in a "love" relationship for your own emotional, physical, or sexual gratification violates love's guideline of protecting and providing. Taking for your own pleasure does not contribute to the happiness, health, and spiritual growth of another person.

*True love will not pressure another person into having sex.* There is tremendous pressure in our culture for students to become sexually active, even in casual dating relationships. Today's movies, music, and the media treat premarital sex as normal and expected. But sex outside God's plan for intimacy in marriage can leave mental, emotional, and spiritual scars for years. True love protects a person from such guilt and pain, and it provides for a secure, nurturing relationship by saying no to premarital sex.

*True love will not insist on an "exclusive" friendship.* Some students become very possessive of a boyfriend or girlfriend's time and attention. Instead of protecting and providing for the other person, this approach restricts and stifles a person's happiness, health, and spiritual growth. True love encourages healthy interaction with others.

*True love will not do anything to damage the happiness, health, and spiritual growth of another person.* So how do you know when you have found true love? You know love is real when you make the happiness, health, and spiritual growth of your boyfriend or girlfriend as important to you as your own. That's what it means to protect and provide for someone you love. The following guidelines will help you integrate this definition into your experience with that special person in your life.

- Put Jesus Christ first in your relationship.

- Be open and honest with each other.

- Accept each other completely, including faults and failures.

- Seek your parents' approval for your relationship.

- Avoid any setting or activity that may tempt you to compromise your commitment to sexual purity.

- Handle disagreements quickly and lovingly.

- Emphasize the "friend" in boyfriend and girlfriend.

It's too soon to tell if Luke and Traci's relationship will end up in a marriage commitment. Many other factors will come into play over the next months and years, particularly God's leading in their college and career decisions. But Luke has turned a corner in his relationship with Traci. He has accepted Doug's challenge to protect and provide for her as long as they are together. This is a no-lose situation for both of them. If Luke and Traci end up getting married in the future, they will begin their life together on the solid foundation of protecting and providing for each other, which is God's kind of love. If they should eventually go their separate ways, they can part with no regrets, having contributed to each other's health, happiness, and spiritual growth.

You may be no more certain about the future with your special friend than Luke and Traci are about theirs. But the prospects for your relationship will be just as bright and positive as you focus on the true love of protecting and providing for one another.

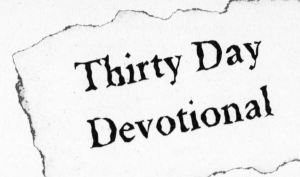

# Thirty Day Devotional

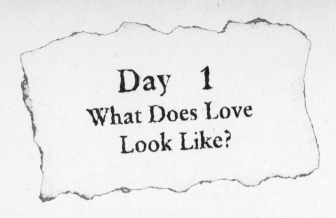

# Day 1
## What Does Love Look Like?

### READ: EPHESIANS 5:25–30

*No one ever hated his own body, but he feeds and cares for it, just as Christ does the church (Eph. 5:29).*

One summer years ago I commuted between a lakeside cabin in the mountains and a conference center down in the valley where the temperatures often reached one hundred degrees. I went down into the valley twice each day to teach Christian leadership classes: once in the morning and again after lunch.

During my trips up and down the mountain, I often saw overheated cars and their frustrated drivers parked on the shoulder of the steep, winding road. I soon realized that this was an opportunity to share the love of Christ with needy people in a very practical way. My summer teaching ministry was rather hollow if I didn't do something to help the stranded motorists. So I devised a plan.

I bought four large water jugs, filled them, and stowed them in the trunk of my car. Whenever I saw an overheated car on my daily journeys on the mountain, I pulled over and offered to fill the radiator with water. People were overjoyed at my offer and very grateful for help from a complete stranger. Once I filled the radiator, I usually offered a copy of my book, *More Than a Carpenter*, and talked to the motorists about Christ. It was one of the most rewarding summers I have ever experienced.

Love for others—family members, friends, a romantic interest, or even strangers—isn't just a warm feeling or a nice thought. True love has substance to it. You should be able to see it in action. What does love look like? I hope the stranded motorists on the mountain road saw love in a friendly smile, a jug of water, and a paperback book. And I hope the love they experienced made a difference in their lives.

Remember the scene when Doug and Luke were at the batting cages? Doug read Ephesians 5:28–29 to Luke and explained, "Paul says we should care for the needs of others just as we do for ourselves. In fact, you can tell that love is real when the happiness, health, and spiritual growth of another person is as important to you as your own." Doug was helping Luke to see what love looks like.

Keep two pictures in mind. First, love nourishes others, providing for their happiness, health, and growth just like we water and cultivate a plant in the garden. Second, love cherishes others, protecting them from danger like a mother bird spreading her wings over her defenseless young. In any relationship, ask yourself, "Am I regarding this person as a tender flower and a defenseless little bird? Am I helping to provide for this person's happiness, health, and growth and to protect him or her from harm? And is this person treating me in the same way?"

That's what true love looks like.

# MY JOURNAL JOURNEY

### REFLECT

"When I think about God's fantastic design for true love, I feel . . ."

---

---

---

### RESPOND

Does your idea and practice of love totally measure up to God's design? If not, what will it take on your part to transform your love to look more like His ideal?

---

---

---

### PRAY

Tell God in writing your heart's desire for nourishing and cherishing others in love.

---

---

---

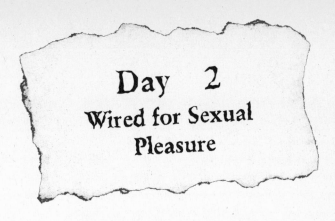

# Day 2
## Wired for Sexual Pleasure

**READ: PROVERBS 5:15–19**

*Rejoice in the wife of your youth. . . . May her breasts satisfy you always, may you ever be captivated by her love (Prov. 5:18–19).*

Your heart is racing. Your mouth is dry. Your palms start to sweat. Your stomach is doing backflips. You feel warm and tingly all over. It's the biggest charge of excitement you have ever felt in your life.

What are you doing? Well, you're either strapped into the front car of the world's wildest roller coaster as it climbs the steep incline, ready to hurtle down the track at ninety miles per hour, or you're holding hands with the most gorgeous person you've seen, anticipating your first embrace or first kiss. Either way, the sensation is about the same. The moment is electric, exciting. It may also be a little scary—but it's a *good* kind of scary. You don't ever want this pleasurable feeling to go away.

Luke and Traci rode this exhilarating roller coaster of intense romantic sensation. They were so into the pleasure of being together that they almost compromised their sexual purity. That's how strong and captivating sexual attraction can be. It feels so good to be close to that special someone of the opposite sex that you just want to get closer, more intimate.

So does that make sexual attraction wrong? Should sexual pleasure be renounced because it could draw you into sexual sin, like the irresistible light that draws moths into the patio bug zapper? In other words, is sexual pleasure sinful?

33

No, sexual pleasure is not sinful. God invented our sexual organs and urges and wired us to enjoy sexual activity to the fullest. If you have any doubts, reread Proverbs 5:18–19 above and check out Song of Solomon in the Bible, a poem celebrating sexual enjoyment between husband and wife. The sexual feelings you are experiencing should serve to remind you that God has designed you for physical, emotional, and spiritual intimacy when the time is right.

When is the time right? God designed sex for marriage. Within the bounds of marriage, there are three reasons for sex: procreation—for the purpose of having children; identification—for the purpose of developing oneness physically, emotionally, and spiritually; recreation—for the purpose of pleasure and enjoyment. Sexual activity is meant to take place between a man and woman who have committed to be united to one another for life, to become one flesh (see Gen. 2:24).

The pleasure that sex provides—the very reason it is so appealing even outside of marriage—is God's creation. When sexual pleasure is experienced in marriage as God designed, the pleasure is maximized. God wired you for sexual pleasure, but He also wants you to maximize the enjoyment He created for you by reserving sex for marriage. It's a thrill ride worth waiting for.

# MY JOURNAL JOURNEY

## REFLECT

When you consider that God created sexual pleasure for you to enjoy when you marry, what does it do to your heart?

_____

_____

_____

## RESPOND

"I will cooperate with God's purpose for sexual pleasure by . . ."

_____

_____

_____

## PRAY

"God, help me prepare for receiving Your wonderful gift of sex by . . ."

_____

_____

_____

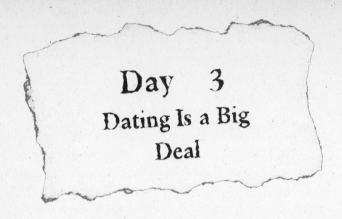

# Day 3
## Dating Is a Big Deal

**READ: JOHN 15:12–17**

*My command is this: Love each other as I have loved you
(John 15:12).*

"Why is it such a big thing," one girl asks, "if I don't have a date?"

"I know I probably shouldn't feel this way," echoes someone else, "but I can't help thinking that if I'm not dating, I'm a zero."

"Why can't I be satisfied with having friends? My friends are important to me, but I really, really want to be special to someone."

These are fair questions, which every student must deal with. Let's examine several factors that make dating such a "big deal" for most young people.

1. Dating is a big deal because you are going through a lot of physical changes that heighten your sense of your sexuality. Dating is a tangible way to find out if someone else notices that you are an attractive, desirable person. That's not to say that all dating is based on physical beauty, but in our appearance-conscious society, it certainly is a contributing factor. We're not kidding anyone if we say that guys and girls aren't attracted to each other for physical reasons. The challenge is to keep physical attractiveness from being the basis for social relationships.

2. Dating is a big deal because it often seems like an approval rating on your personality. Our culture links desirability to dating. TV ads play on this theme a lot. The girl who dresses

right, has her hair fixed just right, and uses the right tanning oil is popular with the guys. When we approach such ideas rationally, we know they are not true. But we don't usually live our lives by logic alone. Our emotions tell us that we want to do all those things—superficial as they may be—that TV and movies and advertising tell us will make us liked by our friends and peers.

3. Dating is a big deal because kids your age are hungry for the affection that comes from being special to someone. God intended for young children to receive big doses of love and affection from their parents. Unfortunately, many parents are either unavailable to their children or they feel uncomfortable giving affection to them. So many kids grow up feeling a powerful need to be cherished by someone else.

4. Dating is a big deal because it meets your need for intimacy. All of us long to share ourselves totally with another person. A dating relationship is a significant way to open up to someone else.

5. Dating is a big deal because you have a healthy longing for social friendships with a person of the opposite sex. You are not weird because you would like to know more about how the other sex thinks. Dating can be a means for satisfying this healthy curiosity.

So if you are longing to date at this stage of your life, it is a good longing. Keep seeking the Lord to help you fulfill this longing in positive ways.

# MY JOURNAL JOURNEY

## REFLECT

"God is really interested in my dating life. This reality prompts me to . . ."

_____

_____

_____

## RESPOND

How do you need to change your view of dating in light of God's interest?

_____

_____

_____

## PRAY

"God, I want to seek Your help in my dating life, specifically . . ."

_____

_____

_____

# Day 4
## Companionship
## at Its Best

**READ: PROVERBS 17:17, 18:24; REVELATION 3:20**

*A man of many companions may come to ruin, but there is a
friend who sticks closer than a brother (Prov. 18:24).*

Behind the idea of dating is our common desire to have a special
friendship with someone. You and I need an intimate, affectionate,
transparent relationship with someone. Fulfilling that need begins
with Jesus. Jesus has all the qualifications to be your perfect "date."
I do not say this to be trite. He embodies everything you could ever
want in a special, intimate friend. Consider the following:

*Jesus seeks your friendship.* Revelation 3:20 reveals that Jesus
desires a special relationship with you . . . a close, personal relationship.

*You are special to Jesus.* No one is common or ordinary to
Jesus. As amazing at it sounds, no one is plain or unappealing to
Him. No matter what you or others see as your personality hang-
ups, your physical flaws, or your intellectual ability, He is fond of
you. No one can ever fill the place that Jesus has reserved for you in
His heart.

*Jesus has affectionate feelings for you.* Jesus is a person with
feelings for you. When you are feeling bummed out, He understands
and cares. When something exciting happens and you are filled with
joy, Jesus is joyful with you. Because He is a feeling God, you can
know that He shares your happiness and sadness. Frankly, it is
probably a disappointment to Him when you don't include Him in
the ups and downs of your life. He is a kind, compassionate, understanding Lord who fully participates in all aspects of your life.

*You can be intimate with Jesus.* No one knows your innermost thoughts and feelings like this wonderful companion. He is delighted when you and I share our most personal thoughts with Him. You can go to your room and pour out your heart to Him, and you can be sure that He listens attentively. You can tell Him your dreams and longings and know that He understands what you mean. When your relationship with your parents is under stress, Jesus is available to listen.

Rather than looking to some special guy or girl as a place of identity and security, we need to look to Jesus Christ as the one friend who will *always* be there for us. What better time than during your teenage years to determine to make Him the one special person in your life?

I am very grateful for a decision I made when I was about eighteen. One day at a summer camp in upstate New York, I told Jesus that I wanted Him to be number one in my life. The friendship with Him that has progressively deepened and become more intimate is perhaps the greatest experience of my life.

It is my prayer that you will be able to experience this friendship of a lifetime.

# My Journal Journey

### REFLECT

"When I consider that Jesus cares deeply for me and wants me as a friend, I sense . . ."

_____

_____

_____

### RESPOND

Is there anything or anyone that hinders your friendship with Jesus? What can you do to better respond to His desire to be intimately involved with you as a friend?

_____

_____

_____

### PRAY

Tell Jesus in your own words what it means to you to be called His friend.

_____

_____

_____

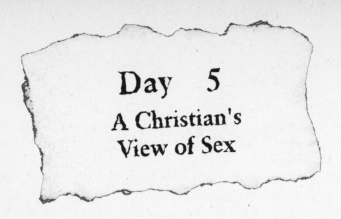

# Day 5
## A Christian's View of Sex

**READ: ROMANS 13:7–10**

*Love does no harm to its neighbor (Rom. 13:10).*

"I grew up in a neighborhood that consisted of about twelve guys, all one to three years older than me," said a young man I'll call Ron. "Every weekend we'd get together to play sports, work on our cars, talk about girls. Every weekend my mind was bombarded with the same general idea about manhood: Real men must be having sex with anyone and everyone. As I continued to listen to the older guys brag about their conquests, I began to fantasize about what it would be like for me."

Ron and many other students like him grew up with some version of the world's view of sex. This view led to Ron becoming sexually active as a teenager, up to the time that he became a Christian. Then he remarked, "I have come to realize my whole life could have been ruined, all because I chose to respond to some false thinking I picked up from other guys way back in junior high."

The Christian's view of sex is different from the world's view of sex. Understanding God's view of sex will help you answer the world's view and stay pure.

First, the Christian believes that each person is special and of great worth because each one is made in the image of God. This means that every individual deserves dignity, respect, and consideration. In practical terms, a guy who lives with a Christian agenda will give dignity, respect, and consideration to his girlfriend.

Second, because each person has great worth, the Christian

believes we should not manipulate people to please ourselves or to get our needs met at their expense. To use people cheapens them. It implies that we think we are better than they are, that they don't deserve any better treatment from us.

Third, a Christian believes that we should treat others with the love and respect God gives to us, the same appreciation we would like to receive from others. What is this love like? Read 1 Corinthians 13:4–8 to find out. These verses describe the way God loves us, and this is the kind of love we want to receive from others. You should therefore give others the same quality of love (Matt. 7:12).

Fourth, a Christian believes in the value of waiting. According to 1 Corinthians 13:4, love is patient. In God's perfect plan for us, there is a proper time and place for everything, including, as Ecclesiastes 3:5 says, "A time to embrace and a time to refrain." The world says, "Are you lonely? Do you feel the need for intimacy? Are you curious about sex? No problem. There is no need to wait until marriage." The Christian answers, "There is a time and a place for sexual intimacy and pleasure, a time and a place that God honors and that is best for us. That time and place is the marriage relationship."

# MY JOURNAL JOURNEY

## REFLECT

What version of sex did you grow up with, the world's view or the Christian's view? How was that view impressed on you?

_____

_____

_____

## RESPOND

"I may need to change my view of sex to match the Christian's view, specifically . . ."

_____

_____

_____

## PRAY

"God, I need Your view of sex in order to stay pure. Please help me to . . ."

_____

_____

_____

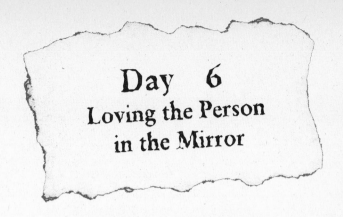

# Day 6
## Loving the Person
## in the Mirror

### READ: MATTHEW 22:34–40

*"Love the Lord your God with all your heart and with all your soul and with all your mind." This is the first and greatest commandment. And the second is like it: "Love your neighbor as yourself" (Matt. 22:37–39).*

Jesus has given us two great love commandments: Love God and love people. Each law was given with a qualifier to help us to know *how* to love at each level. Jesus commanded us to love God "with all your heart and with all your soul and with all your mind." As for loving others, Jesus instructed, "Love your neighbor as yourself." Our love for others is to be patterned after our love for ourselves.

"Wait a minute!" someone may argue. "The Bible commands us to deny self and take up our cross. Jesus said if I love my life, I will lose it. Self-love is right up there with pride and conceit, things we are to avoid."

OK, there is a problem with a me-first, who-cares-about-you?, selfish self-love. But a proper self-love is right for at least three biblical reasons.

First, it is right to love ourselves because we are made in God's image (Gen. 1:26). We also love others for this reason, especially certain individuals who seem lovable for no other reason. We must love ourselves as God's creation even in those discouraging moments when we don't feel we are worth loving.

Second, it is right to love ourselves because self-love is the basis for loving others. Had Jesus said, "Love others *instead of* loving yourself," then any kind of self-love would be wrong. But He commanded us to love others *as* we love ourselves. It's as if Jesus said, "You already love yourself, and to do so properly is good. Now love others the same way."

Third, it is right to love ourselves because God loves us (1 John 4:10). If we do not love ourselves, we do not love what God loves, and it's never a good idea to oppose God. It is normal and necessary for believers to nourish themselves to maturity—mentally, physically, spiritually, and socially—and to protect themselves from harmful elements. This loving regard for ourselves is the pattern for our love for others.

The two dangers of self-love are *over*loving yourself and *under*-loving yourself. You probably love yourself too little if, when your boyfriend compliments how you look, you point out one of your flaws instead of saying thanks. You probably love yourself too much if you dominate discussions with your girlfriend because you're convinced she doesn't know as much as you do. If we undervalue or overvalue ourselves, we are less fit to love others as Christ has commanded us.

A healthy, balanced self-love and a respectful attention to nourishing ourselves to maturity and protecting ourselves from damaging influences best equips us to love others as we love ourselves.

# My Journal Journey

## REFLECT

How do you react to the thought that God expects your love for others to be patterned after your love for yourself?

_____

_____

_____

## RESPOND

"If I am to love others as I love myself, my self-love needs to change in these ways . . ."

_____

_____

_____

## PRAY

Write down your own words of praise and thanks for God's work in helping you to love yourself and others.

_____

_____

_____

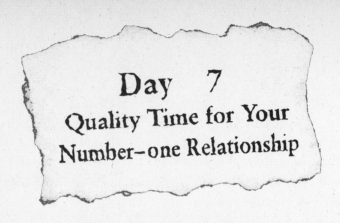

# Day 7
## Quality Time for Your Number–one Relationship

### READ: HEBREWS 10:19–25

*Let us draw near to God with a sincere heart in full assurance of faith (Heb. 10:22).*

Several years ago I conducted a little experiment. I kept track of how much time I spent in the bathroom each day. Then I compared that with the amount of time I spent each day trying to get to know Jesus better. The results were a bit embarrassing. Counting showers, fixing my hair, brushing my teeth, and so on, I spent an average of sixty minutes a day in the bathroom. But on average I gave Jesus only five to eight minutes a day. The result was that I knew my bathroom fixtures much better than I knew God! It was time to begin putting more effort into knowing Jesus better.

Building a love relationship with God is different from building a friendship with someone else. There is one thing, though, that is absolutely necessary for both: time. Spending time with God is an absolute necessity in building a loving friendship with Him. Many people call their time with God a quiet time. I prefer to call it *quality time*. I'm confident that if you spend quality time with Jesus every day, it will make an impact on your relationship with God and with others.

I suggest you try what is known as 5-5-5 Quality Time with God. It requires about fifteen minutes each day. A daily 5-5-5 time is an easy way to strengthen your friendship with God.

First, spend five minutes in prayer. Prayer is simply talking to God. Begin by telling God what you appreciate and admire about

Him and why you love Him. Move on to confession of sin, asking God to forgive you for ways you have let Him and others down. Thank Him for all He does for you. Then ask God for help in specific areas of your life and the lives of others. Close your prayer by reaffirming that you will trust Him no matter how He decides to answer your requests.

Second, spend five minutes reading the Bible. As you read, look for verses that seem to be written just for you. Believe that the Lord wants to speak to you through the Bible. Expect that He will have something to say to you each time you read.

Third, spend five minutes worshiping God. Worship is the activity of giving glory to God. One of the most common forms of worship is singing. If you have any favorite worship songs, I recommend that you take this time to sing a few. Another way I like to worship is by listening to worshipful music on my CD player. I close my eyes and let the words and music help me praise God.

The best thing about spending 5-5-5 Quality Time with Jesus each day is that your friendship with Him doesn't stop when the fifteen minutes are over. Your devotional time is a means to help you to recognize and depend on Him throughout the whole day. And before long you may want to spend increasing amounts of quality time with Him each day.

# MY JOURNAL JOURNEY

## REFLECT

Describe any thoughts or feelings stirring within you about your relationship with God.

_____

_____

_____

## RESPOND

How would you like to change your pattern of daily devotions after today's reading?

_____

_____

_____

## PRAY

"Lord, when I think about drawing closer to You daily, I ask . . ."

_____

_____

_____

# Day 8
## Sharing the Gold in the Golden Rule

### READ: PHILIPPIANS 2:1–11

*Each of you should look not only to your own interests, but also to the interests of others (Phil. 2:4).*

True love demands that we care as much for the success, happiness, and growth of others as we do for ourselves. Love simply says, "Treat others right, the way you want to be treated." It all goes back to the Golden Rule given to us by Jesus: "In everything, do to others what you would have them do to you" (Matt. 7:12).

How does this definition play out in everyday life? Here are a few examples.

- If you talk your little brother into finishing your household chores so you can go on a date with a special guy, love requires that you do your brother's chores when he needs some time off.
- If you think your youth leader should be more attentive to your spiritual needs, love requires that you do your part to meet his or her needs, such as praying for your youth leader on a regular basis and sharing an encouraging Scripture verse occasionally.
- If you expect your boyfriend or girlfriend to pick you up on time, love requires that you be ready on time.

The loving thing to do in most situations is not difficult to discern. Simply put yourself in the shoes of the people involved and ask yourself, "What is the best I could wish for if it were me?" When you determine the answer, love requires that you do the best that you have the opportunity and ability to do. When you do this, you are following the example of the God of love. God wills only the best for every person, as seen in His deeds.

First, He created us in His image and likeness (Gen. 1:27). He could have made us in the image of angels or other beautiful creatures. But His best for us was that we reflect His nature. What better model could we ask for than to be formed in God's image and crowned with His glory and honor (Ps. 8:5)?

Second, God wills the best for us by sustaining our life on this planet through His loving power (Col. 1:16–17). We owe our daily existence to the God who sustains us as an ongoing expression of His love.

Third, God demonstrated that He wills the best for sinful humanity by redeeming us at great cost. When Jesus Christ died on the cross, He did so for all people (2 Cor. 5:15), even those who never respond to His love.

The love we are commanded to express in all our relationships is to be given with no demand for return. That means doing your brother's chores even if he won't do yours, being ready for a date on time even if your boyfriend or girlfriend is always late. That's the way we look to the interests of others. That's the way we love.

# My Journal Journey

### REFLECT

"When I realize that God loves me completely even if I did not love Him in return, I feel . . ."

_____

_____

_____

### RESPOND

"In order to follow God's example of wanting the best for others, I need to . . ."

_____

_____

_____

### PRAY

Write your words of thanks for God's love and your prayer to follow His example of love.

_____

_____

_____

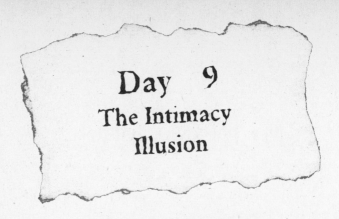

# Day 9
## The Intimacy Illusion

### READ: GENESIS 2:18–25

*The LORD God said, "It is not good for the man to be alone.*
*I will make a helper suitable for him" (Gen. 2:18).*

All of us long to share ourselves totally with another person, as Adam and Eve did in the Garden. That's true intimacy: sharing every part of your life with someone else. You desire someone who will love and accept you for who you are, someone you can open up to without fear of rejection. In God's design for man and woman, the ultimate expressions of intimacy are reserved for marriage. Yet dating relationships are the place where you begin to develop intimacy with someone of the opposite sex.

You have a built-in desire for love and intimacy, but you probably don't know how to find it. You may feel drawn to an illusion of "instant intimacy." The seemingly quickest, easiest way to intimacy is through sex. But sexual intimacy alone can never fulfill your deepest needs. You see, intimacy involves more than physical closeness or sexual involvement. In fact, intimacy may take many forms, such as

- mental intimacy: sharing new discoveries, ideas, and insights that are challenging or exciting.

- emotional intimacy: sharing those things that are emotionally exciting or discouraging, both highs and lows.

- spiritual intimacy: sharing new steps of spiritual growth, new discoveries in spiritual reality, questions, fresh conversations with God.

- crisis intimacy: going through difficulties together, giving and receiving support.

- goal intimacy: setting common goals and pursuing them together.

One student expressed her understanding of intimacy this way: "As I view my relationship with my fiancé, our most special times are when we have excellent conversations. Kissing is great enjoyment, but we have found intimacy through conversations, talking about intimate things as well as working through problems. It sounds dull, but it's not."

Intimacy in dating relationships is built on trust. Trust is built over time, with a lot of communication as you work through problems. You see that the other person isn't going to "dump" you. You know that he or she is committed to you. Trust is established, and trust leads to vulnerability, and that leads to transparency, and that results in intimacy—closeness to another person.

As your relationship with that special person in your life grows, set your sights on developing intimacy at all levels. It is not good for your special friend to feel alone.

# MY JOURNAL JOURNEY

## REFLECT

What do you appreciate about God's design to remove your loneliness through intimacy with others? What questions does God's design bring to your mind?

_____

_____

_____

## RESPOND

"If I am to be God's instrument for providing intimacy to others, I must . . ."

_____

_____

_____

## PRAY

"God, my greatest need in learning to love others intimately is . . ."

_____

_____

_____

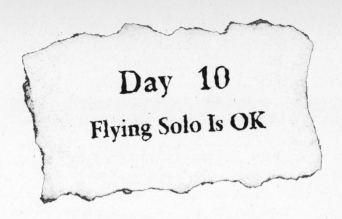

# Day 10
## Flying Solo Is OK

**READ: 1 CORINTHIANS 7:25–35**

*I wish that all men were as I am. But each man has his own gift from God; one has this gift, another has that (1 Cor. 7:7).*

It wasn't like she had never had any offers. Susan was popular and pretty. She had more than her share of dates. She was a member of the homecoming court in high school. She was fun to be around, and she was real cute. But Susan graduated from college at age twenty-two with no wedding ring, no engagement ring, not even a serious boyfriend.

That's when the comments started: "Why are you waiting so long to get married?" "Why hasn't someone snatched you up yet?" "Don't you think it's time to grow up and settle down?" "You're not getting any younger, you know." "Maybe it's time to stop looking for Mr. Perfect and settle for Mr. Good Enough."

Some people wondered if there was something wrong with Susan. She knew they all meant well, but she quickly became tired of their questions and comments about her being single. "I know a lot of people think I'm some sort of freak because I'm still single. But I don't want to get married because someone else thinks I should. I want it to be because I've found someone to love for the rest of my life. I'm willing to wait forever, if I have to, to find that kind of love."

There's nothing wrong or freaky about being single, either temporarily or for a lifetime. Jesus, Paul, John the Baptist, and many others in the Bible were not married, and no one can question their impact on the world. And there are certain benefits enjoyed by people who are not married. Here are just a couple of them.

First, you don't have the hassles of a busy family life. Taking care of one person is a lot easier than taking care of two or more. You can come and go as you please, make your own decisions, and so on. Yes, there are many benefits to being married. But for as long as you are "flying solo," you have a certain amount of freedom that married persons no longer have.

Second, you have more time to serve God. Your schedule is your own. You can take off on a short-term (or long-term) missions trip without having to worry about leaving someone behind or arranging for two to go. You can donate more time, energy, and money to your church because you don't have to share it with anyone else.

If you are a little concerned whether you will eventually marry, put your concerns in God's hands. He knows you and your future, and His plans for you will bring you ultimate joy. In the meantime, make the most of the freedom and flexibility you enjoy at this special time in your life.

# MY JOURNAL JOURNEY

## REFLECT

"The thought of being single for a large part of my life—or all of it—makes me feel . . ."

_____

_____

_____

## RESPOND

What minor or significant changes need to take place to help you prepare for remaining single for as long as God determines?

_____

_____

_____

## PRAY

Express to God in your own words your heart's desire concerning your future as either a single or married person.

_____

_____

_____

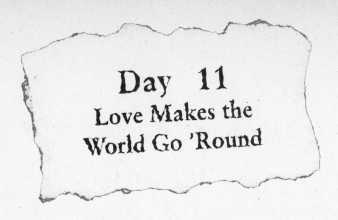

# Day 11
## Love Makes the World Go 'Round

### READ: 1 JOHN 4:7–16

*Dear friends, since God so loved us, we also ought to love one another (1 John 4:11).*

Everyone wants it. Without it, life would be, at best, incomplete—at worst, desperate. The yearning to give and receive love throbs in the heart of everyone, male and female alike. Luke and Traci were both quietly convinced that they had found love. But had they?

From beginning to end, the Bible shows us God's definition of love, the only accurate definition available. Unfortunately, since our culture has lost sight of God, we have also lost the understanding of love. As a general rule, we have reduced love to one of two things: (1) a warm feeling or emotional reaction or (2) a positive response to a relationship that makes us feel good. Both of these views of love are self-directed, not other-directed, and they conflict with the Bible's definition of love. No wonder students today become confused about love.

Understanding what love is starts by understanding God's number-one word for love in the Bible: *agape*. It's the Greek word translated "love" in today's Bible passage. Authors Stacy and Paula Rinehart define true love with the biblical term *agape*:

Agape love is an unconditional response to the total person: "I love you in spite of" (the weaknesses I see in you). [It is a] concern for the welfare of someone without any desire to control that person, to be thanked by him, or to enjoy the process. It reaches beyond to a "willingness to give when the loved one is not able to reciprocate, whether it be because of illness, failure, or simply an hour of weakness. It is a love that can repair bonds severed by unfaithfulness, indifference, or jealousy." The best example of this type of love is God himself. "For God so loved the world that he *gave*" (John 3:16).[1]

Luke was shocked and saddened to discover that his girlfriend Traci had contracted multiple sclerosis. But it is situations like these—when life is less than ideal, when people are less than perfect—that allow agape love to shine through. The fact that Luke stayed and promised to help Traci through the difficult days ahead is a clue that there is something more to his love than just warm feelings and sexual desire.

Don't get me wrong: Warm feelings and sexual desire for someone are part of the package we call love. But as strong as they may be, feelings and desires are not the heart of love. Selfless caring and serving without expecting or demanding a return is what agape love is all about. Go straight to the heart of love by experiencing agape love in your relationships.

# MY JOURNAL JOURNEY

### REFLECT

"As the recipient of God's 'I love you in spite of' love for me as a
total person, I am moved to say . . ."

———————————————————————————

———————————————————————————

———————————————————————————

### RESPOND

What do you feel is your next step of growth in becoming an "agape
lover"?

———————————————————————————

———————————————————————————

———————————————————————————

### PRAY

Write your own words of love and adoration to the God who loves
you completely today.

———————————————————————————

———————————————————————————

———————————————————————————

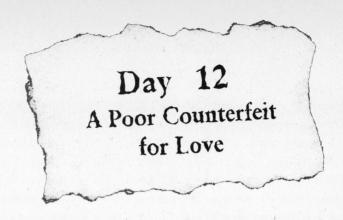

# Day 12
## A Poor Counterfeit for Love

**READ: 1 JOHN 2:15–17; GALATIANS 5:19–23**

*For everything in the world—the cravings of sinful man, the lust of his eyes and the boasting of what he has and does—comes not from the Father but from the world (1 John 2:16).*

Dear Josh:

When I was only fourteen years of age, I dated an eighteen-year-old boy. After a month or so of dating, he told me that he loved me and had to "have me." He said that if I loved him, I would have sex with him. And if I wouldn't, he couldn't control his desire for me and would have to break up with me.

What did I think at fourteen years of age? I knew sex was wrong before marriage, yet I so desired to have a man love me. I was so insecure in my father's love and had a poor self-image. So here was my boyfriend who I really liked (and thought I loved), telling me he loved me. Well, I needed that love. So I finally gave in.

I felt so guilty afterward. I can remember sobbing in my bed at night after I'd come home from being with my boyfriend. I wanted so much to have my virginity back. I began to feel so lonely inside, and yet there was no one I could turn to.

As this girl discovered, there is a big difference between love and lust in a relationship. Today's Scripture passages pinpoint the stark contrast. True love comes from God, but lust—a counterfeit that is sometimes passed off as love—is the product of a godless world and sinful human nature. Lust leads to sexual immorality, impurity, and debauchery (see Gal. 5:19–20), which the Bible categorizes with idolatry, witchcraft, hatred, discord, rage, and so on. Love keeps company with joy, peace, patience, kindness, goodness, faithfulness, gentleness, and self-control (see Gal. 5:22–23). Notice some other contrasts between lust and love:

- Love goes into a relationship to give what the other person needs. Lust goes into a relationship to get what it wants from the other.

- Love respects, values, and cherishes the other person. Lust regards the other person as something to be used for its own gain and pleasure.

- Love is steady, persevering, and enduring no matter what the circumstances. Lust flashes hot and cold depending on what it wants at the moment.

- Love is the fruit of those who walk in the Spirit. Lust is a hallmark of those whose eyes are more on this world than on God.

Don't settle for a cheap imitation. Hold out for the real thing—true love—in your relationships.

# My Journal Journey

## REFLECT

If you could talk to the girl whose letter you just read, what would you say to her? How would you describe your feelings about love and lust?

_____

_____

_____

## RESPOND

"I need to move more in the direction of true love in my relationships by . . ."

_____

_____

_____

## PRAY

"Help me, Lord, to grow in love and get rid of lust in my life. I especially need Your help when . . ."

_____

_____

_____

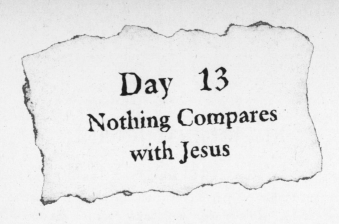

# Day 13
## Nothing Compares with Jesus

### READ: PSALM 23:1–6

*The LORD is my shepherd, I shall not be in want (Ps. 23:1).*

Friendships are as varied as flowers. Some are beautiful, yet delicate. Others are hearty—they'll grow anywhere. In Texas where I live, some flowers thrive in the blistering summer heat. Others start out fine in the spring but quickly wilt when the temperature begins to rise.

You and I have one totally unique friendship that stands apart from all others—our friendship with Jesus Christ. As great as your other friends may be, none can compare with Jesus. He is an all-weather, all-circumstances friend.

First, Jesus is a *full-time* friend. He will always be there for you. He doesn't treat you one way when you're alone and another way when others are around. You can count on Him to be consistent, loving, warm, and open forever.

Second, He is the one *unconditional* friend who will always forgive you when you fail Him. He will stick with you through whatever circumstances occur in your life. When the going gets tough, Jesus will be by your side. David, the writer of the twenty-third Psalm, said, "Even though I walk through the valley of the shadow of death, I will fear no evil, for you are with me" (v. 4).

Third, Jesus is fully *dependable*. You don't need to be afraid that He will mock you, turn His back on you, or betray your confidence. And He will keep His word. You can count on His promises to be more certain than the fact that the sun will rise tomorrow.

Finally, Jesus, the ultimate friend, is never superficial or trite. He wants a *significant* relationship with you. He bares His heart to you and treats you with compassion and tenderness when you bare your heart to Him. The Bible gives many examples of His compassion toward those who were physically disabled, socially outcast, or in emotional grief. Those examples are actual demonstrations of His intense, personal care for others.

I'm also impressed that Jesus was not a stiff, formal person. Common people were not uncomfortable in His presence. He could chat with Zacchaeus over lunch. He could have an intimate conversation with the Samaritan woman at the well about her failed marriages and present living condition. One of His disciples, John, could put his head on Christ's shoulder at mealtime and feel loved and accepted. If Jesus treated these people this way, He'll do the same for you and me.

We have one great, faithful, unconditional friend—Jesus Christ. Let's learn to take our disappointment, loneliness, and hurts to Him—along with our excitement, happiness, and fun events—and experience the friendship that will last for eternity. Let's really get to know our friend.

# My Journal Journey

## REFLECT

How do you feel knowing that Jesus is committed to being your friend through all circumstances?

_____

_____

_____

## RESPOND

How can you help others experience the friendship you enjoy with Jesus?

_____

_____

_____

## PRAY

"Jesus, I want to grow as a faithful, loving friend to You. Help me to do that by . . ."

_____

_____

_____

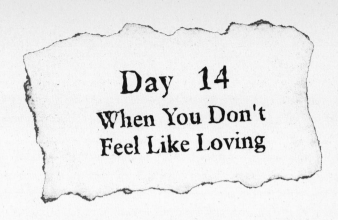

# Day 14
## When You Don't Feel Like Loving

**READ: JOHN 13:34–35; 1 JOHN 3:16–23**

*Dear children, let us not love with words or tongue but with actions and in truth (1 John 3:18).*

Love—the word slips into our conversations almost unnoticed every day.

- "Don't you just love it?"
- "I heard a great story; you'll love it!"
- "My kitten is so cute. I just love him."
- "You gotta love our team!"

Turn on the radio or TV anytime day or night. You can't get away from love. It is crooned on music stations, dramatized in soap operas, humorized in sitcoms, and mocked in trash-talk shows.

- "Love can't be wrong if it feels so right."
- "If you can't be with the one you love, love the one you're with."
- "What the world needs now is love, sweet love."
- "I want your love; I need your love (O baby, baby, baby)."

Even as Christians, we talk a lot about love: love for God, love for one another, love for the lost, and so on. And sometimes we feel all warm and loving toward someone. Contrary to popular opinion, love is more than a good feeling. The key to true love is to obey God by loving others "with actions and in truth" beyond mere feelings of devotion.

Whether with a romantic partner, a family member, a classmate, a neighbor, or a stranger, ask yourself: Is the health, happiness, and growth of this person as important to me as my own? Am I ready to protect this person from any elements that will threaten his or her well-being or hinder his or her growth? And, most important, am I demonstrating my love in practical ways even when I don't feel like it?

Jesus didn't feel like giving His life to redeem humankind (Matt. 26:38–39). On the night before His crucifixion, Jesus was in agony in the garden. He asked the Father if there was any way He could avoid the cross. But He loved the Father and yielded to His will, and He loved us and became the sacrifice for our sin. That's how we are to love. We act on the basis of our obedience and love for God, who commands us to love others as He has loved us.

The bonus for us as we begin to love people when we don't feel like it is that eventually we can learn to feel good about it too. When we do the right thing by loving "with actions and in truth," we can learn to like doing it. Good feelings often follow right, loving choices.

# MY JOURNAL JOURNEY

## REFLECT

"When I think about Jesus' commitment to die for me even when He didn't want to go to the cross, I feel . . ."

_____

_____

_____

## RESPOND

"I want to grow in my love for those I don't feel like loving, but that means I need to . . ."

_____

_____

_____

## PRAY

Write your words of praise and petition to God on the topic of loving others even when you don't feel like it.

_____

_____

_____

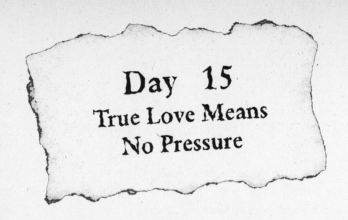

# Day 15
## True Love Means No Pressure

### READ: 1 CORINTHIANS 13:1–8

*[Love] always protects, always trusts, always hopes, always perseveres. Love never fails (1 Cor. 13:7–8).*

If the words "I love you" are not followed immediately by a period, you may be dealing with a subtle counterfeit of true love. I'm not talking about how to punctuate a sentence. I'm talking about how to tell if what you *think* is love—or what someone else *claims* is love—is really true love. One of the quickest ways to spot a counterfeit is to see if there are any strings attached to the words "I love you." Here are some common examples:

- "I love you for always being so kind to me."
- "I love you because you're so cute."
- "I love you because you go out with me."
- "I love you because you are such a good listener."
- "I love you because you bring me nice presents."

This isn't true love; it's conditional love—which isn't the kind of love the Bible talks about. When you relate to someone on the basis of conditional love, you are always on the bubble. What happens if you don't act so kind or if you don't look so cute or if you can't go out with the person or . . . ? What happens to the other person's love when the favorable conditions go away? Love goes away too. True love has a period at the end: I love you, period—even when you are unkind or not listening or can't go out. It's love without strings. That's biblical love.

Here is another set of statements that reveal conditional love:

- "If you love me, you will prove it."
- "If you love me, you will spend all your time with me."
- "If you love me, you won't go to camp without me."
- "If you love me, you will have sex with me."

I call these "pressure lines," not love lines. The true nature of love is seen in how we treat people, not in what we demand from them. The result of pressure lines is that the person being pressured begins to feel that his or her behavior or compliance is the test of true love. In reality, the true test of love is found in 1 Corinthians 13. You can recognize whether someone loves you by the way that person protects you, trusts you, seeks the best for you, shows patience toward you, and hangs in there with you through less than ideal conditions. If someone loves you, he or she will respect your feelings and not push you into doing something you are not ready for.

# My Journal Journey

## REFLECT

How do you evaluate your love for others in light of these paragraphs comparing conditional and unconditional love?

_____

_____

_____

## RESPOND

Write about the steps you need to take to help you focus on loving others unconditionally.

_____

_____

_____

## PRAYER

"Lord, thank You for loving me unconditionally. Help me to learn to love like You do, especially in situations like . . ."

_____

_____

_____

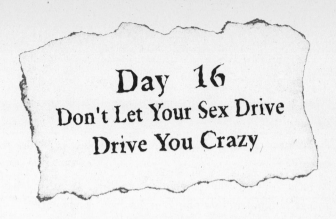

# Day 16
## Don't Let Your Sex Drive Drive You Crazy

### READ: 1 CORINTHIANS 6:9–20

*You are not your own; you were bought at a price. Therefore honor God with your body (1 Cor. 6:19–20).*

How do you harness your God-given sex drive? How do you temper the "urge to merge" when you know sexual activity is to be reserved until after marriage? Luke and Traci had to deal with this issue after their passionate evening outside the observatory. Our Scripture passage today provides two helpful answers.

First, remember to whom your body—with all its sexual desires and capabilities—belongs. As a Christian, your body belongs to God, the one who bought you with a costly price by dying on the cross for you (see 1 Pet. 1:18–19). You wouldn't think of borrowing your father's nice car and then entering it in a demolition derby down at the local race track. It's not your car, so you don't have the right to trash it and return it to Dad on a tow truck. Similarly, since you belong to God, you don't have the right to trash your body through illicit sexual activity. It belongs to Him, so He alone has the right to say what you do with it.

Second, honor God with your body by setting high standards for how you use it in dating relationships. Here is what a number of Christian students just like you have discovered and stated regarding the importance of honoring God by setting sexual standards:

- "Sexual desires are practically impossible to harness once let loose. It is important to stop the process before it begins."

- "Set your standards. Write down what you will and will not do on a date."

- "You must determine where you want to end . . . before you begin."

- "I have to live by my own convictions, and for me this has meant setting strict standards in the area of purity."

- "Draw a line that you will not cross over. Define those areas you think are restricted to marriage. Consider these areas off limits."

- "Don't test your limits. Don't play games with sexuality. Don't experiment to find out how far you can go without sinning. Set limits and stick to them."

Remember: The time to look for a fire escape is before the building catches fire. Daniel found this to be true. When faced with the overwhelming odds of compromising his moral convictions, this young person had already decided what he would do: "Daniel made up his mind that he would not defile himself . . ." (Dan. 1:8 NASB).

Someone has said, "It is much easier to break *no* standard than it is to break *some* standard. Don't just slide; decide!" If you wait to set your standards until your hormones are aroused, you are probably too late.

# MY JOURNAL JOURNEY

### REFLECT

"When I realize that my body belongs to God, I feel . . ."

_____

_____

_____

### RESPOND

Write about the standards you want to set in order to honor God with your body.

_____

_____

_____

### PRAY

"Lord, it's my desire to let You determine how I use my body. I ask You to . . ."

_____

_____

_____

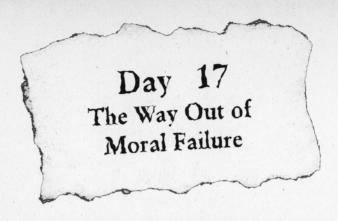

# Day 17
## The Way Out of Moral Failure

### READ: PSALM 51:1–13

*Create in me a pure heart, O God, and renew a steadfast spirit within me (Ps. 51:10).*

King David is a good example of someone who failed morally. He was the king of Israel, God's hand was on him, he had everything going for him. Then he saw Bathsheba and let his thoughts and desires cross over the line. The Bible says, "David sent messengers to get her. She came to him, and he slept with her" (2 Sam. 11:4). Bathsheba became pregnant as a result. Since the woman's husband, Uriah, was off in battle, David decided he had to get Uriah home so that he would think the child was his own. But Uriah was so committed to the king that he would not go to bed with his wife while he was supposed to be in battle. And so David devised a plan in which Uriah was killed.

When the prophet Nathan confronted the king, David confessed his sins and received God's forgiveness. We must do the same whenever we break God's laws. God has promised to forgive us, even for moral failures and sexual sin.

Here are several steps to take when you sin:

1. Acknowledge your sin. A lot of people say, "God, I have sinned, but . . ." and offer an excuse like "I loved her" or "I'm not strong enough." Just say, "God, I have sinned." Admit your sin without excuses.

2. Change your behavior. Matthew 3:8 says, "Produce fruit in keeping with repentance." Repentance means turning around, changing your mind and behavior. This might mean breaking off an unhealthy relationship or making a decision not to be alone together or limiting future physical contact.

3. Acknowledge Christ's forgiveness. God has promised to forgive confessed sin (1 John 1:9). Christ's forgiveness can make you whole again.

4. Forgive yourself. You may feel that you can't forgive yourself for such a failure. God's forgiving grace is extended to us out of His heart of love. If we do not forgive ourselves, we throw God's grace right back into His face. God's grace covers moral sin because God's grace covers all sin.

5. Don't let Satan deceive you. Satan, the great deceiver, will try to make you feel condemned for what you did. But if you are trusting Jesus Christ as your Savior, you are not condemned (Rom. 8:1). Be sure to discern the difference between condemnation and conviction. When sin enters your life, the Holy Spirit convicts you to draw you to Christ, forgiveness, and joy. But Satan's condemnation pulls you away from Christ and leads you to despair. If you feel condemned and worthless, that's Satan trying to keep you under a cloud. Resist him in Christ's name, and he must go.

# MY JOURNAL JOURNEY

### REFLECT

"When I think of God's willingness to forgive King David's adultery and murder, I feel . . ."

_____

_____

_____

### RESPOND

Examine your heart. What secret sins—perhaps even some of a sexual nature—need to be dealt with?

_____

_____

_____

### PRAY

Write your prayer of confession and repentance. Be sure to include your thanks to God for totally forgiving you.

_____

_____

_____

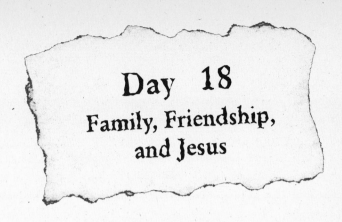

# Day 18
## Family, Friendship, and Jesus

### READ: PSALM 46:1–11

*God is our refuge and strength, an ever-present help in trouble (Ps. 46:1).*

All of us have the need to belong. I believe that the Lord intended that need to be met first by our families. No matter how hostile the world is, I can always come home, kick off my shoes, and say, "I can be myself here." It's a good feeling when your home is a safe, relaxing, friendly place. Unfortunately, a large number of students today don't experience this. For them, home is a lonely place—not really *home*.

Jesus knew what it was like not to have a home. His brothers and sisters were not exactly excited about His ministry. They might even have thought He was an embarrassment. In addition, as He traveled throughout Israel for the last three years of His earthly life, He didn't have a home. Where did He turn for a sense of belonging? Better yet, *to whom* did He turn?

Jesus had a confident sense of belonging to His Father. Like us, He couldn't see the Father, but He knew His Father was with Him and this gave Him a peace and security that sustained Him. That kind of relationship is pictured beautifully in Psalm 46. Later on, the psalmist says, "Lord, you have always been our home" (Ps. 90:1 TEV).

So you see, Jesus *can* live in your home, even if He finds your family members absent or difficult to get along with. He is secure in His Father's love, He has strength to live in a less-than-perfect situation. And that's the clue for you and me to succeed. Jesus wants us to take Him into our home and to be at home with Him. If you read through the first four books of the New Testament, which tell about Jesus when He was here on earth, you will find Him constantly visiting people's homes and welcoming people into His life.

When we are at home, Jesus wants us to know that He is literally there with us (Rev. 3:20). He wants to talk with us, and He wants us to talk with Him, like two close friends sitting across the table, eating and visiting.

As we learn to enjoy Jesus' friendship at home, home becomes a less lonely place. We also begin to be more peaceful inside ourselves because Christ makes us more at ease, more relaxed with our circumstances, whatever they might be. People around us may not change, but we discover that we have a close, personal friend who is changing us.

# MY JOURNAL JOURNEY

## REFLECT

Write about your home and how you feel about being there. What
do you think about Christ's offer to live in your home?

_____

_____

_____

## RESPOND

How can you better experience and appreciate Jesus' presence with
you in your home?

_____

_____

_____

## PRAY

Tell God about your concerns and joys at home. Ask Him to help
you to include Him there. Thank Him for His love for you and
your family.

_____

_____

_____

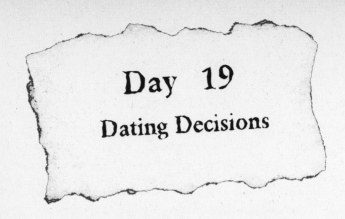

# Day 19
## Dating Decisions

### READ: 2 CORINTHIANS 6:14–18

*Do not be yoked together with unbelievers. For what do righteousness and wickedness have in common? Or what fellowship can light have with darkness? (2 Cor. 6:14).*

Who should you date? To start with, I strongly suggest you, a Christian, avoid dating non-Christians. I have several good reasons, based on today's Scripture passage.

First, everyone you date is a possible (though perhaps remote) candidate for marriage. Since you will marry someone you date, it makes sense that the people you date meet the most basic requirement of a marriage partner—being a Christian.

Second, even if there is no intention of marriage, a non-Christian doesn't share your convictions and standards. Yes, there are some very moral non-Christians. But even if their intentions are good, their convictions may not be as strong as yours, and dating them can lead to immorality.

Third, get below the surface when evaluating your potential dates. Looks and popularity are superficial and don't really say anything about a person. Even personality doesn't reveal much about important inner qualities, such as character and convictions.

When you do find someone you feel good about dating, I think it's a good idea to set some standards for your dates. Here are several to think about.

1.  Write out some goals for dating. Having fun and getting to know the other person are good goals. But additional goals for

honoring God and your date will lead to a more enjoyable time and help to keep you from moral compromise.

2. Begin each date with prayer. Commit your time together to the Lord. It will set the right tone for a date and remind you both of your relationship with God and of His presence with you during the date.

3. Choose dating activities that provide good opportunities for conversation. Talking together is the best way to get to know someone. A movie or concert limits conversation. Activities like hiking, throwing a Frisbee at the park, or riding bikes together allows time to talk.

4. Avoid places, circumstances, and activities where temptation to immorality is likely. This might include attending parties where drugs or alcohol will be available or going to movies with strong sexual content. And avoid being alone together for too long. Spend your time in public places or on group dates.

5. Keep your relationship focused on aspects other than the physical. Get to know each other intellectually, emotionally, and spiritually. I'm not saying there should be no physical contact. But, as they say, "Don't light a fire you can't put out." In other words, don't start something physically that you will be unable to stop.

Treat every date the way you hope others will treat the person you will marry. And keep in mind that the person you date may be someone else's future husband or wife.

# My Journal Journey

## REFLECT

How do you feel about the dating guidelines shared above and how they apply to your relationships?

_____

_____

_____

## RESPOND

Write about any adjustments you need to make in your dating relationships.

_____

_____

_____

## PRAY

"Lord, I want to honor You in my dating activities. Help me to do so by . . ."

_____

_____

_____

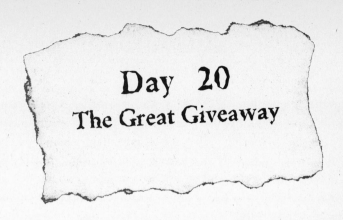

# Day 20
## The Great Giveaway

READ: EPHESIANS 5:1–10

*Live a life of love, just as Christ loved us and gave himself up for us as a fragrant offering and sacrifice to God (Eph. 5:2).*

In his book *The Four Loves,* the late C. S. Lewis, who also wrote the classic Narnia series, calls the Bible's agape love "gift-love." It is the love that gives to another without demand for return. It is the love that makes the health, happiness, and growth of others as important to us as our own. It is the love that is committed to provide and protect, to contribute to an individual's purity. God's gift-love was supremely demonstrated in the gift of His Son for our redemption. Gift-love is to characterize all our relationships: families, dating relationships, friends, classmates, strangers, even our enemies.

But if you think that the gift-love we are to exercise is a lame, use-me-for-a-doormat kind of love, consider the further implications of agape.

First, *true love involves discipline* (Heb. 12:6). True love does not go soft on wrongdoers and let things slide. Love confronts those who are out of line—a friend who shoplifts when you are at the mall together, a date who wants you to compromise your moral purity, a dishonest boss—because such love will ultimately protect that person from the painful consequences of his or her behavior. Love accepts the offender while firmly rejecting the offense.

Second, *true love can be tough.* Jesus, God's love in the flesh, displayed His anger at His opponents (Mark 3:5), verbally blasted hypocrites (Matt. 23), and physically expelled the greedy merchants from the temple (John 2:12–24). Love for your friend may require you to confront him or her about cheating on an exam, possibly risking your friendship. Love for a date may demand that you decide to go home early if whatever you are doing violates your stand as a Christian. Divine love is patient and kind, but it is anything but spineless. True love can be tough when necessary in order to protect and provide.

Third, *love can fail*. The proper translation of 1 Corinthians 13:8 is not "Love never fails" but "Love never ends." The sad truth is that not everyone is won over by love. God loved Adam and Eve fully and perfectly in the Garden, but His love failed to prevent them from choosing to sin. We must exercise gift-love with the realization that our efforts may fail to make a difference in the ones we love. However, the old saying applies well to divine agape: It is better to have loved and lost than never to have loved at all. Jesus loved and lost one of His apostles (John 17:12). And He loved the whole world (John 3:16), but many will be lost (Matt. 7:13–14). Don't let a lack of response from some discourage you from sharing God's love with everyone.

# MY JOURNAL JOURNEY

### REFLECT

"Realizing that true love may involve discipline and confrontation and may fail to be returned, I feel . . ."

_____

_____

_____

### RESPOND

"When my love for others does not match up with the gift-love described above, I need to . . ."

_____

_____

_____

### PRAY

Write to God about your application of gift-love in your closest relationships.

_____

_____

_____

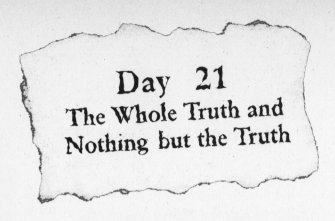

# Day 21
## The Whole Truth and Nothing but the Truth

### READ: EPHESIANS 4:25–32

*Therefore each of you must put off falsehood and speak truthfully to his neighbor, for we are all members of one body (Eph. 4:25).*

Remember the scene from the story when Traci's mom tearfully explained to her the sobering details about multiple sclerosis? Her mom said, "It's a disease of the central nervous system, honey, attacking the brain and spinal cord. They don't know the cause, and they don't know the cure. Depending on the locality of the disease, it can produce . . . disabilities."

Naturally, Traci was shocked and stunned—and very afraid—at the news. Wouldn't you be? She was facing the possible eventual loss of use of her legs, arms, speech, or other physical abilities. Worse yet, Traci learned that MS is eventually fatal. What a terrible emotional blow for a beautiful high school girl.

The story goes on to say that Traci went outside to wait for Luke, who was on his way over to help her buy and install a car battery. She wondered how Luke would take the news of her recently discovered disease. She really liked Luke—in fact, she was pretty sure that genuine love was at the core of her feelings for him. Would Luke break up with her when she told him about her disease? Traci was momentarily tempted not to tell him anything. Why would she want to reveal something that might turn him away?

What if Traci had kept her news from Luke in an attempt to keep him? What if she had decided not to tell Luke until she was sure he would love her anyway? Would that have been fair, honest, truthful? Eventually, Luke would have found out, of course. But how would he feel about being misled? How would you feel if you were Luke?

Truth and honesty are vitally important ingredients in any loving relationship, including a dating relationship. Paul instructed us to speak truthfully to our neighbor. Your "neighbor" is not just the person who lives next door. A neighbor can be anyone: family members, friends, classmates, boyfriend or girlfriend, or even a stranger. In all our relationships, truthfulness and honesty is the "neighborly" thing to do.

So when you can't go out on a date—or don't want to go out—should you make up some excuse or be honest about the real reason? When you are with your boyfriend or girlfriend, should you make everything in your life sound perfect, or should you also be honest about some of your struggles and difficulties?

Traci didn't want to tell Luke about her MS, but she did because it was right. It was also a loving act, sparing Luke from the pain of hearing her news from someone else, giving him the opportunity to process her news and deal with it. There is no guarantee that your honesty will always be welcomed as Traci's was. But God will honor your truthfulness and honesty in the face of the temptation to do otherwise.

# My Journal Journey

### REFLECT

"As I think about being truthful and honest in my relationships, I realize that . . ."

_____

_____

_____

### RESPOND

Are you aware of any ways you have been less than completely truthful or honest in a relationship? If so, what will you do to change?

_____

_____

_____

### PRAY

"Lord, fill me with Your truth and righteousness so that I may . . ."

_____

_____

_____

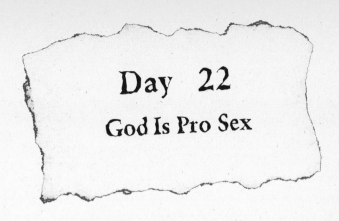

# Day 22
## God Is Pro Sex

**READ:** JAMES 1:12–17

*Every good and perfect gift is from above, coming down from the Father of the heavenly lights, who does not change like shifting shadows (James 1:17).*

Why is premarital sex wrong? The answer begins with an understanding of the character of God. God is not a intergalactic killjoy bent on ruining our fun. He didn't create us to enjoy sex only to frustrate us by severely limiting how we experience it. Rather, God designed us and made us, and He knows what is best for us. Everything He plans for us is for our good (Deut. 10:13). Today's verse reminds us that God is the giver of every good gift we enjoy. So when He says that sex is reserved for marriage, He isn't restricting our fun; He's showing us the best way to enjoy sex. God isn't trying to keep us from having a wonderful sex life; He's giving us positive instruction on how to have the most wonderful sex life possible.

Suppose a world-class hurdler trained sacrificially for four long years to get ready for the Olympics. But when he showed up for his race, he found that there were no lanes marked to keep the runners from crashing into each other. What if the hurdles were scattered all over the track and there was no finish line to designate the end of the race. The race would be total chaos, ruining the competition and endangering the safety of all the participants.

An Olympic event must be set up and managed by someone who knows what is best for the race and the competitors. In the same way, we need someone in our lives who knows what is best for us and lovingly sets boundaries for our provision and protection. Fortunately for us, God did so before we even asked Him to, primarily in His Word, the Bible. The reasons for saying no, based on the Bible, make sense.

1. God protects and provides for us physically. He protects us from sexually transmitted diseases like AIDS, from unwanted pregnancy and abortion, and from sexual addiction. He provides for us a marriage relationship with no guilt.

2. God protects and provides for us spiritually. He protects us from His judgment, from an interrupted walk with Him, and from being a poor influence on others. He provides the blessings of purity, growth of patience and trust, and His fellowship.

3. God protects and provides for us emotionally. He protects us from guilt, from the hardships of breaking up, from psychological and emotional distress, and from a poor self-image. He provides for us the richness of maturity, the affirmation of dignity, and the beauty of only one "first time."

4. God protects and provides for us relationally. He protects us from comparing people as sex partners, from sex dominating love in relationships, and from damaged family relationships. He provides the beautiful relationship found only in marriage. God is saving the best for you if you save yourself for marriage.

# MY JOURNAL JOURNEY

## REFLECT

"When I consider God's reasons for reserving sex until marriage, I feel . . ."

_____

_____

_____

## RESPOND

Where do you most feel the need for God's provision and protection sexually? Consider the four categories above and write your response.

_____

_____

_____

## PRAY

Write a psalm of praise to God for His loving provision and protection for you.

_____

_____

_____

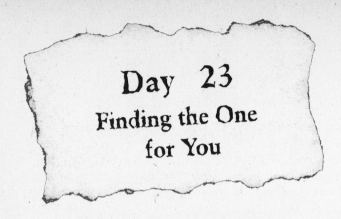

# Day 23
## Finding the One for You

**READ: COLOSSIANS 3:12–17**

*Let the peace of Christ rule in your hearts, since as members of one body you were called to peace (Col. 3:15).*

Bible teacher Charles Swindoll writes, "Success in life consists not so much in marrying the person who will make you happy as in escaping the many who could make you miserable."[2] Many students approaching high school graduation agonize over choosing the "right" marriage partner, and of course, this is an important decision. In order to help you let the peace of Christ rule in your heart on this important issue, consider carefully these three questions.

1. Is there only one right person? Some Christians firmly believe that God has only one person for you to marry. Others believe that you can marry any one of a number of people. Perhaps the place to start is by looking for *a* right person instead of *the* right person. The following four questions are the bare minimum requirements. If you hope to take a godly path toward marriage, all four must be answered yes.

   • Are you both Christians? (See 2 Cor. 6:14.)

   • Have you sought God's will about your relationship in a biblical manner?

   • Do you love each other with biblical love? (See 1 Cor. 13.)

   • Do your parents approve of your relationship? (See Exod. 20:12.)

   This narrows down the field considerably. From within this group, you can be confident that God has someone for you.

2. How do I know I have found the right person? Like many decisions, the choice of a husband or wife will affect the rest of your life—actually, the rest of two people's lives. And, like any effort to discern God's will, it should be considered prayerfully and biblically. But once you have sincerely sought God's guidance regarding the choice of a mate, how do you know if the right decision has been made?

   Author Tim Stafford offers a helpful perspective: "You know the right one for sure on the day you stand in front of the preacher and say 'I do.' Until that day you probably won't know for sure. After that day the issue is settled forever."[3] So the key to finding the right person is how you prepare for that day.

3. How do I prepare? Once it is clear that you have found the person you will marry, the next steps are engagement and marriage. The engagement period should give enough time to prepare for the big event. Many counselors suggest a minimum of three to six months. But the engagement should not last so long that the temptation to sexual activity becomes unmanageable. In most cases, an engagement should last no more than a year.

# MY JOURNAL JOURNEY

## REFLECT

"All this talk about finding someone to marry makes me feel . . ."

_____

_____

_____

## RESPOND

Write about where you are, and where you would like to be, on the journey of finding the right person for your life.

_____

_____

_____

## PRAY

"Thinking about marriage, Lord, I need Your peace in my heart because . . ."

_____

_____

_____

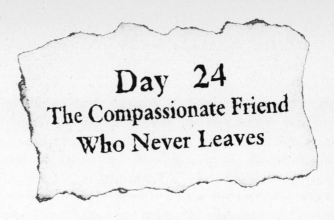

# Day 24
## The Compassionate Friend
## Who Never Leaves

### READ: ROMANS 8:31–39

*For I am convinced that neither death nor life, neither angels nor demons, neither the present nor the future, nor any powers, neither height nor depth, nor anything else in all creation, will be able to separate us from the love of God that is in Christ Jesus our Lord (Rom. 8:38–39).*

Here is a great truth that keeps all other relationships in proper perspective: Jesus, who loves you unconditionally, is the one friend you will never lose. Every other relationship will end someday through changes, moves, breakup, or death, but Jesus will *always* be there.

Isn't that exciting? Doesn't it give you great hope and encouragement to know that nothing can separate you from His unconditional love? He will never get tired of you. He will never "break up" with you because He found someone better. He will never say, "That's it—I'm leaving!"

But there's more. Jesus is a warm compassionate friend who is with you when you go through the loss of your earthly friends, including the breakup of romantic relationships. Jesus was a friend to Mary and Martha when their brother, Lazarus, died (John 11). The Bible specifically says that Jesus loved Mary, Martha, and Lazarus. When He heard of Lazarus's death, He went to be with the two sisters. As He came to Mary, He noticed that she and her friends were weeping in grief. Jesus was deeply moved by what He saw and He began to weep, too, touched by their loss.

When I was a young Christian, I was taught that the Lord was too perfect to associate with our human feelings. For years, I felt that He was a stainless-steel God—radiant, pure, invincible . . . but without feeling. But then as I read the Bible and got to know Jesus for myself, I made a startling discovery. I found out that Jesus has feelings. Not only that, I saw He has feelings *for me!* I found, with great delight, that a favorite word to describe Jesus when He was on earth was "compassionate." Over and over again I noticed the Bible saying that Jesus had compassion for people. His love is not some impersonal, abstract, emotionless thing; Jesus is a warm, tender, gentle, kind, and sensitive Savior.

That's exactly the kind of friend He is to you and me. This powerful truth has challenged me to get to know Him better and better. And now I want Jesus to be your best friend so that when all other relationships fail, fade, or are cut off, your friendship with Him will support you through those difficult times. You'll know that you're not alone. You'll have Him to share your most personal feelings and your most intimate thoughts. What a friend!

# MY JOURNAL JOURNEY

### REFLECT

Write your thoughts and feelings about a God who will never leave you no, matter what you do or what happens to you.

_____

_____

_____

### RESPOND

"Knowing God will never leave me, I want to celebrate and honor my loyal, loving friend by . . ."

_____

_____

_____

### PRAY

Tell God in writing what kind of friend you want to be to Him.

_____

_____

_____

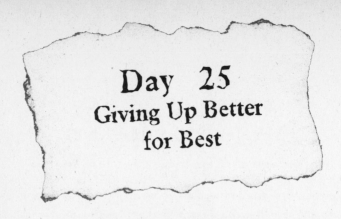

# Day 25
## Giving Up Better for Best

### READ: PSALM 84:1–12

*For the LORD God is a sun and shield; the LORD bestows favor and honor; no good thing does he withhold from those whose walk is blameless (Ps. 84:11).*

A devastating sense of loneliness and loss often occurs when a close dating relationship ends. The pain is most intense when the relationship is called off by the other person. You feel devastated, fearing no one will ever love you again.

I remember when one of my close relationships disintegrated. I loved Paula, and I thought she was everything I wanted in a wife. We'd been going together for more than three years. Yet God wouldn't give me peace about our relationship.

My uneasiness became so intense that I knew I had to share my feelings with Paula. We sat together in a Mexican restaurant as I reluctantly shared my anguish and doubt about our relationship. When I finished, she admitted that she had been having the same feelings, but she had kept them to herself because of her love for me. Finally, with tears and a nagging fear of the unknown, we decided to break off our relationship, believing that if God meant for us to be together, we couldn't stay apart.

The next morning, as my plane rolled away from the terminal where I had kissed her good-bye, I thought my heart would break. I was angry at God. I prayed, "God, how can You be so unloving, so uncaring?" I let it all out. "If You are a loving God," I said, "why are You taking Paula from me?" This went on for about an hour in the back of the plane. I cried in front of everyone.

Then, when I was at the point of emotional exhaustion, God began to get through to me when Psalm 84:11, quoted above, gripped me. Suddenly I realized that God wasn't taking Paula out of my life to make me miserable but because He desires the best for me. "Then the woman you give me will be better than Paula?" I questioned God. That didn't seem right. God seemed to say, "Not necessarily *better* than her, but *better for you* than her."

It wasn't until several years later that I fully appreciated what God had done for me. When I met and married Dottie, I knew that God had reserved His best for me. If I had stayed with Paula, I would have never experienced the awesome love and incredible relationship that Dottie and I share.

We don't always know what's best for us. And sometimes it's painful to give up what we think we want, someone we think we must have. But God has better things in mind for us. He knows us better than we know ourselves. And He always wants us to have the best, *His* best!

God wants to meet your needs. It will still probably hurt like crazy when love leaves, but if He's withholding something or someone from you, it's because He has something better in mind.

# MY JOURNAL JOURNEY

## REFLECT

"Josh's story reminds me of the pain I experienced in losing a relationship, namely . . ."

_____

_____

_____

## RESPOND

"I may need to change the way I view a lost relationship, focusing more on . . ."

_____

_____

_____

## PRAY

Tell God how you feel about trusting Him for His best for you.

_____

_____

_____

# Day 26
## You Don't Know Love If You Don't Know God

### READ: 1 JOHN 4:7–16

*God is love. Whoever lives in love lives in God, and God in him (1 John 4:16).*

In *Mortal Lessons: Notes on the Art of Surgery,* Dr. Richard Selzer tells of his encounter with a young woman after he removed a tumor from her face. Surgery required the severing of a facial nerve, leaving one side of her mouth lifeless and crooked. The surgeon was concerned about how the woman and her husband would respond to her new appearance. The doctor writes:

> Her husband is in the room. He stands on the opposite side of the bed, and together, they seem to dwell in the evening lamplight. . . . The young woman speaks. "Will I always be like this?" she asks. "Yes," I say. "It is because the nerve was cut." She nods and is silent. But the young man smiles. "I like it," he says. "It's kind of cute" . . .
>
> He bends to kiss her crooked mouth, and I am so close I can see how he twists his own lips to accommodate hers, to show that their kiss still works. . . . I hold my breath and let the wonder in.[4]

How do you think that husband felt about his wife's new deformity and unsightly appearance? Disappointed? Sad? Probably all that and more. How difficult it must have been for him to see his wife so disfigured and realize she would be that way the rest of her life. How could his love for her remain strong in light of her condition?

Let's get even closer to home. How would you feel if the special person in your life was disfigured in an accident or was diagnosed with a crippling disease? How could you continue to love that person when his or her physical appearance or ability changed?

To love someone when something about that person is unlovable is beyond us. Love is something we need and something we need to express, but love is not our basic nature. Love is something we *have*, not something we *are*. Love resides within us and operates through us by the presence of the Holy Spirit, but its source is beyond us.

Love never changes. Therefore the ultimate source of love must be as changeless as love itself. As Christians, we identify our changeless God as the source of love. The apostle John wrote, "God is love." In contrast to His human creation, God does not *have* love; He *is* love. God's activity of love flows from His nature of love. When God loves, He is simply being Himself.

So how can we love someone when it seems impossible to love? It can't happen apart from the knowledge of the God of love. We can't know love without knowing God, who is love. The command to love means nothing unless we know what love is, and the meaning of love is rooted in God.

# My Journal Journey

## REFLECT

Consider the phrase, "We can't know love without knowing God, who is love," and write your thoughts and feelings about this truth.

_____

_____

_____

## RESPOND

"Realizing I must know God if I am to know love, I need to . . ."

_____

_____

_____

## PRAY

"God, You are love, and I praise You for . . ."

_____

_____

_____

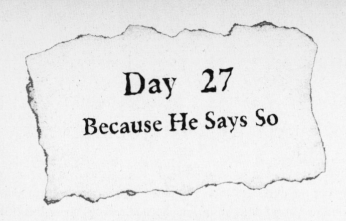

# Day 27
## Because He Says So

**READ: 1 THESSALONIANS 4:3–8**
*It is God's will that you should be sanctified: that you should avoid sexual immorality (1 Thess. 4:3).*

You wouldn't believe how some adults try to scare kids into staying sexually pure. Here are some crazy reasons for avoiding premarital sex given by parents, teachers, ministers, and other well-meaning adults. There may be a grain of truth in some of them, but they are usually used to just scare kids into right behavior:

- If you have sex before marriage, your sex organs will fall off.
- God will get you because premarital sex is an unforgivable sin.
- You think you're doing it in secret, but everybody in heaven will see you.
- God will curse you with AIDS or some other sexually transmitted disease.
- Once you start having sex, you won't be able to stop.
- If you have sex before marriage, you won't enjoy sex once you *are* married.
- Premarital sex causes serious acne.
- If you get pregnant, the child will be born with serious emotional problems.
- Once people know you have had sex, you won't be able to get a date.

- You can kiss your dream of a happy marriage and family good-bye.

God's reason for His children remaining sexually pure until marriage is a lot less complicated and not at all frightening. As today's Scripture passage states, it is simply God's will that we avoid sexual immorality—which is any sexual activity outside of marriage. Everywhere I go students ask me how they can know God's will for their lives. In some areas, God's will is often difficult to discern. But in the area of sex, it couldn't be any plainer. He just says don't do it before you're married.

Now if it rubs you the wrong way to hear God say, "Because I say so," you may need to adjust your focus. You may be focusing too much on the rule and not enough on the one who gives the rule. Remember, God is the one who loves you more than anyone else can possibly love you. He's the one who knows all about you—your faults as well as your strengths—and accepts you unconditionally anyway. He's the one who allowed His Son to die on the cross so you could enjoy a loving relationship with Him for eternity. More than anyone else, God has your best interests at heart.

Would someone who loves you this much ask you to do anything that wasn't for your good? Would He say no just to spoil your fun or frustrate you? The better you get to know Him, the more you will understand that His will regarding sexual purity is just another way He expresses His love for you.

# My Journal Journey

### REFLECT

Write your thoughts and feelings about God's clear will concerning sex.

_____

_____

_____

### RESPOND

How is your attitude toward God's will in this area? What kind of attitude adjustment, if any, do you need to pursue?

_____

_____

_____

### PRAY

"Thank You, God, for making Your will so plain in this area. It makes me feel . . ."

_____

_____

_____

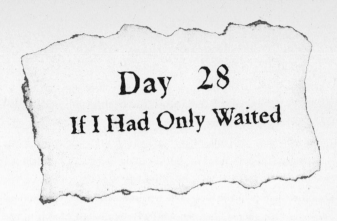

# Day 28
## If I Had Only Waited

### READ: PHILIPPIANS 1:1–11

*And this is my prayer: that your love may abound more and more in knowledge and depth of insight, so that you may be able to discern what is best and may be pure and blameless until the day of Christ" (Phil. 1:9–10).*

There's a battle raging today for your body and soul, and you are on the front line. It's a battle between what the Bible says love is—regarding the health, happiness, and growth of others as highly as you do your own—and what the world says love is—self-gratification and sexual freedom. Sexually transmitted diseases, unwanted pregnancies, guilt, and relationship breakdown are just some of the results awaiting those who fall into the world's trap.

My desire is that you never have to make the statement this young person did.

If only I had waited. I see now how uncluttered my life would have been, how my mind would have been free from this burden that besets me even years later.

If you want to know what it is really like, get two pieces of paper and glue part of one to the other. After it has dried, pull them apart. What you have in your hand is vivid picture of two people after a premarital sexual relationship—both torn, both leaving part of themselves with the other. All my relationships had two things in common: one was we made love a lot, and the other was that they always ended and I always went through (and am still going through) incredible pain.

I finally got a girl into bed (actually it was in a car) when I was seventeen. I thought I was the hottest thing there was, but then she started saying she loved me and started getting clingy. I figured out that there had probably been a dozen guys before me who thought they had "conquered" her, but who were really just objects of her need for security. I finally dumped her, which made me feel even worse, because even I could see she was hurting. I didn't feel very cool after that. I felt pretty low.

I gave no thought to what I would tell my future wife about those months when my girlfriend and I engaged in all those pleasures of the marriage bed with none of the commitment. A wife was a nebulous figure in the far-off future, not a person with feelings or someone who would care that I had been intimate with anyone besides her.

Along with the apostle Paul, I pray that you may be able to discern what is best and that you may be pure and blameless until Christ comes again.

# MY JOURNAL JOURNEY

## REFLECT

"After reading this student's statement, I feel . . ."

_____

_____

_____

## RESPOND

"Reminded that I am engaged in a battle, I realize I must . . ."

_____

_____

_____

## PRAY

Write the prayer in Philippians 1:9–10 in your own words, personalizing it to your own life situation.

_____

_____

_____

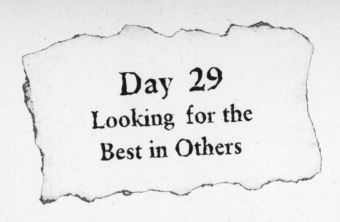

# Day 29
## Looking for the Best in Others

### READ: ROMANS 12:9–18

*Be devoted to one another in brotherly love. Honor one another above yourselves (Rom. 12:10).*

Whenever I talk to students about love in their relationships, I always encourage them to make the happiness, health, and growth of others as important to them as their own. Another way to summarize true love is to always seek what is best for the other person. When I say this, I am sometimes asked, "How can we know what is best for someone else?" Well, you can't know what is best for every person in every situation. But there are some guidelines that can help you discern the best for people in most situations.

First, put yourself in their shoes. What is the best possible good you would hope for in the situation? Once you answer that question, do to others as you would have them do to you.

Second, consider the Scriptures. The more you know about God's Word, the better prepared you are to guide people into healthy, productive behavior.

Third, recall your experience as a Christian. Lessons you have learned the hard way may help you to guide others to the best while avoiding unnecessary disappointment and pain.

Fourth, seek the counsel of mature Christians. Proverbs 15:22 says, "Plans fail for lack of counsel, but with many advisers they succeed."

Fifth, trust the guidance of the Holy Spirit. In every situation, ask God to show you His best for another's life.

Be aware, however, that even when you have the best for others at heart, you cannot force your guidance upon them. Everyone is responsible for his or her own life. You may want to express your love to a friend, for example, by protecting her from the consequences of premarital sex. You know abstinence is in her best interest. You can counsel her and pray with her, but she has to choose the best *for herself;* you can't choose it for her. And if your efforts fail and your friend makes a wrong choice, you are not to blame. If people reject your love, it doesn't mean that you have failed to love. You can only offer to provide and protect; people must choose to accept your offer.

# MY JOURNAL JOURNEY

### REFLECT

"When I try to do what is best for someone, and that person rejects my attempt and gets hurt or gets in trouble, I feel . . ."

_____

_____

_____

### RESPOND

Write about ways you can seek the best for a special friend, even if he or she does not respond.

_____

_____

_____

### PRAY

"Thank you, God, for pouring out Your best to me. When I consider Your generous love, I . . ."

_____

_____

_____

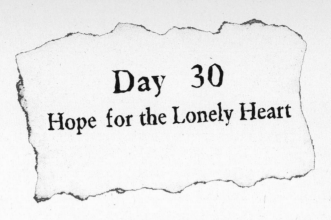

# Day 30
## Hope for the Lonely Heart

**READ: EPHESIANS 5:11–20**

*Be filled with the Spirit (Eph. 5:18).*

Julie lays her cheek against the cold flatness of a study hall desk and wishes everything would just go away. *Everyone knows Brad broke up with me. They don't say so, but I can see them looking at me. Why don't they mind their own business? None of them knows how I feel. None of them cares.* She lifts her head for a moment and then presses the other cheek to the desk and closes her eyes. *I feel so alone.*

Julie's experience is painfully common to students who have been hurt in a dating relationship. Perhaps you have felt very alone like she does. Maybe you feel that way now. Jesus knows what it's like to be lonely, and He did something about it. He provided a constant companion, counselor, and encourager in the person of God's Holy Spirit. You see, when you trusted Jesus Christ as Savior and Lord, you received a colossal "power potential" through the Holy Spirit. Maybe you have yet to tap into that enormous potential.

Something wonderful happened to the Lord's disciples on the day of Pentecost. They were filled with the Holy Spirit and went out in His power to change the course of history. That same Holy Spirit who empowered the disciples to live powerful, fruitful, holy lives can do the same thing today for you. Here's how you can plug in to such incredible power.

First, you must be hungry for God and want to be filled with His Spirit (Matt. 5:6).

Second, you must be willing to surrender the direction and control of your life to Christ (Rom. 12:1–2).

Third, confess every known sin in your heart and experience the cleansing and forgiveness that God promises (1 John 1:9).

Once you have met God's conditions for heart preparation, pray a prayer like the following:

> Dear Father, I need you. I acknowledge that I have been in control of my life and that, as a result, I have sinned against You. I thank You for forgiving my sins through Christ's death on the cross for me. I now invite Christ to take control of the throne of my life. Fill me with the Holy Spirit as You commanded in Your word. I pray this in the authority of the name of the Lord Jesus Christ. As an expression of faith, I now thank You for filling me with Your Holy Spirit and for taking control of my life. Amen.

The Holy Spirit is waiting to fill you, dispel your insecurities, and empower you to live an exciting, rewarding life—fulfilled, because you're Spirit-filled.

# MY JOURNAL JOURNEY

## REFLECT

Write your thoughts and feelings about God making His Holy Spirit available to you.

_____

_____

_____

## RESPOND

"The areas of my life in which I most need the Spirit's power exercised are . . ."

_____

_____

_____

## PRAYER

Close your journal with a prayer of thanks for all God has done in the last thirty days.

_____

_____

_____

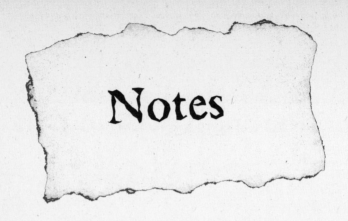

# Notes

1.  Stacy and Paula Rinehart, *Choices: Finding God's Way in Dating, Sex, Singleness, and Marriage* (Colorado Springs, Colo.: NavPress, 1982), 139. The quoted passage is from Robert K. Kelley, *Courtship, Marriage, and the Family* (New York: Harcourt, Brace, Jovanovich, 1974), 214.

2.  Charles R. Swindoll, *Singleness* (Portland, Oreg.: Multnomah Press, 1981), 13.

3.  Tim Stafford, *Worth the Wait: Love, Sex, and Keeping the Dream Alive* (Wheaton, Ill.: Tyndale, 1988), 106.

4.  Quoted in Max Anders, *30 Days to Understanding the Bible* (Dallas: Word Publishing, 1994), 120.

# Connecting Youth in Crisis

This PROJECT 911 Collection is eight small books, each dealing with a specific crisis that many youth encounter. Created in a fictional, though real-to-life format, the collection covers tough issues that often contribute to a young person's relational disconnect. These books employ a "read-it-and-give-it-away" strategy so you can offer "911 help" to a person struggling with one of these issues.

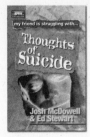

# Experience the Connection

# For Youth & Youth Groups

This eight-week youth group experience will teach your youth the true meaning of deepened friendships—being a 911 friend. Each lesson is built upon scriptural teachings that will both bond your group together and serve to draw others to Christ.

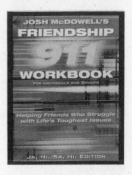

This optional video is an excellent supplement to your group's workbook experience.

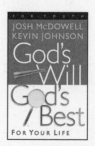

As follow-up to your youth group experience, continue a young person's friendship journey by introducing them to a thirty-day topical devotional journal and a book on discovering God's will in their life.

# Experience the Connection

# If I Had Only Waited

JOSH MCDOWELL, internationally known speaker, author and traveling representative of Campus Crusade for Christ, International, has authored or coauthored more than fifty books, including *Right from Wrong* and *Josh McDowell's Handbook on Counseling Youth*. Josh and his wife, Dottie, have four children and live in Dallas, Texas.

ED STEWART is the author or coauthor of numerous Christian books. A veteran writer, Ed Stewart began writing fiction for youth as a coauthor with Josh McDowell. He has since authored four suspense novels for adults. Ed and his wife, Carol, live in Hillsboro, Oregon. They have two grown children and four grandchildren.